# Free

by Simon Bowen

NT
TRANS
FORM
AT!ON

# TRANSFORMATION

## 29 April–21 September 2002

The Lyttelton *Transformation* project is vital to my idea of the
National Theatre because it both celebrates and challenges our
identity. What do we want the National to be? We must draw on
our heritage, on our recent past, and on the talent of the next
generation. I want a thriving new audience, including a body
of young people under 30 with a theatre-going habit, a new
generation of artistic and administrative talent committed to
taking the National forward and a realization of the varied
potential within this glorious building.

**Trevor Nunn** Director of the National Theatre

*Transformation* is thirteen world premieres, hosted in two new
theatre spaces, with special low ticket prices. The National's most
traditional auditorium, the Lyttelton, has been transformed by
a sweep of seats from circle to stage to create a new intimacy
between actor and audience. At the same time the Loft has been
created – a fully flexible 100-seat theatre. *Transformation* will
introduce new generations of theatre makers and theatre
audiences to one of the most exciting theatres in the world.

**Mick Gordon** Artistic Associate
**Joseph Smith** Associate Producer

*Transformation* has received major creative input from the Studio –
the National Theatre's laboratory for new work and its engine
room for new writing – and celebrates the Studio's continuing
investment in theatre makers.

# Free

## by Simon Bowen

*In order of speaking*

| | |
|---|---|
| Kate | NICOLA WALKER |
| Sophie | CATHERINE McCORMACK |
| Danny | PAUL WYETT |
| David | IAN REDFORD |
| Alex | ANDREW LINCOLN |
| Nick | STEPHEN BERESFORD |
| Chris | DYLAN BROWN |
| Ben | LAURENCE MITCHELL |

| | |
|---|---|
| Director | THEA SHARROCK |
| Designer | RACHEL BLUES |
| Lighting Designer | PETE BULL |
| Sound Designer | RICH WALSH |
| Company Voice Work | PATSY RODENBURG & KATE GODFREY |

| | |
|---|---|
| Production Manager | Katrina Gilroy |
| Stage Manager | Emma B Lloyd |
| Deputy Stage Manager | Thomas Vowles |
| Assistant Stage Manager | Mary O'Hanlon |
| Assistant to the Designer | Keith Baker |
| Projection Realisation | Sven Ortel & Dick Straker |
| Costume Supervisor | Frances Gager, assisted by Louise Bratton |
| Casting | Wendy Spon |

OPENING: Loft, 23 May 2002

Copies of this cast list in braille or large print are available at the Information Desk

**STEPHEN BERESFORD**

NICK

**Theatre:** *Time and the Conways* (Royal Exchange Manchester), *The Rivals* and *Rookery Nook* (Salisbury), *Twelfth Night* (Liverpool Playhouse), *Our Country's Good* (Young Vic/world tour), *Shopping and Fucking* (Royal Court), *Woyzeck* (Gate), *Design For Living* (English Touring Theatre), *Charley's Aunt* and *French Without Tears* (Palace, Watford), *Woman in Mind* (Theatre Royal, York) and *Dracula* (Cheltenham Everyman). **TV/Film:** *Casualty*, *Where There's Smoke*, *History File*, *The Bill*, *Reunion*, *Spring Awakening*.

**DYLAN BROWN**

CHRIS

Dylan Brown trained at Drama Centre. **Theatre** includes *Accomplices* (Sheffield Crucible), *The Changeling* (NT Studio), *Making It Better* (Criterion) and *Beggar's New Clothes* (Cockpit). **TV:** *Dream Team*, *Peak Practice*, *Casualty*, *The Bill* and *Overlanders*. **Film:** *Broken Wings*, *In Between*, *Maddest Man* and *The Mystery of Dr Martino*.

**ANDREW LINCOLN**

ALEX

Trained at RADA. **Theatre** includes *Blue/Orange* (National), *Hushabye Mountain* (Hampstead) and *Sugar, Sugar* (Bush). **TV:** *Teachers* (2 series), *Drop the Dead Donkey*, *N7*, *Overhere*, *Bramwell*, *This Life* (2 series), *Woman in White*, *Bomber* and *A Likeness in Stone*. **Film:** *The Jury*, *I Know the Place*, *Boston Kick Out*, *Human Traffic*, *Offending Angels* and *Gangster No. 1*. **Radio:** *Private Wheeler's War*, *Weird Tales*, *From the Slip of Paranoia* and *As You Like It*.

**CATHERINE McCORMACK**

SOPHIE

**Theatre** credits include *All My Sons* (National), *White Horses* (Gate, Dublin), *Lie of the Mind* (Donmar Warehouse), *Kiss Me Like You Mean It* (Soho) and *Anna Weiss* (Whitehall). **TV:** *Armadillo*, *Deacon Brodie*, and *Frenzy*. **Film:** *Spy Game*, *Tailor of Panama*, *Born Romantic*, *The Weight of Water*,

*Shadow of the Vampire*, *The Debtors*, *This Year's Love*, *Dancing at Lughnasa*, *Land Girls*, *The Honest Courtesan*, *Braveheart* and *Loaded*.

**LAURENCE MITCHELL**

BEN

Trained at Drama Centre. **Theatre** includes *Time and the Conways* (Royal Exchange), *Afore Night Come* (Young Vic), *Accomplices*, *Mr England*, and *Six Degrees of Separation* (Sheffield Crucible), *Troilus and Cressida* (Oxford Stage Co.), *Never the Sinner* (Library), *Filumena* (Piccadilly), *The Doctor's Dilemma* (Almeida) and *Cause Celebre* (Lyric Hammersmith). **TV:** *Kavanagh*.

**IAN REDFORD**

DAVID

**Theatre** includes: *Mother Clap's Molly House* (NT), *Shopping and Fucking*, *Our Country's Good*, *Some Explicit Polaroids*, *Rita, Sue and Bob Too*, and *A State Affair* (Out of Joint); *Chapter 2* (Gielgud Theatre), *M Butterfly* (Shaftesbury), *Who Killed Hilda Murrell?* (Royal Court), *Irish Eyes and English Tears*, *The Plague Year*, *William*, *Built on Sand*, *Agamemnon's Children* (Gate Theatre). **TV & film** includes: *House of Elliot*, *Second Sight*, *The Great Escape*, *Three Men and a Little Lady*, *Remains of the Day*, *ID*, *Prince and the Pauper*, *Antonia and Jane*.

**NICOLA WALKER**

KATE

**Theatre** includes *Dead Eye Boy* (Hampstead), *Sexual Perversity in Chicago* (Sheffield Crucible), *A Lie of the Mind* (Donmar), *Passion Play* (Donmar and Comedy), *Fifty Revolutions* (Whitehall), *Sweetheart*, *The Libertine/The Man of Mode*, *Hated Nightfall* (all Royal Court), *The Lovers* (Gate Theatre). **TV:** *People Like Us*, *Dalziel and Pascoe*, *Jonathan Creek*, *Touching Evil* series 1-3, *A Dance to the Music of Time*, *Moll Flanders*. **Film:** *Shiner* and *Four Weddings and a Funeral*. **Radio:** *The Big Town All Stars*, *Witch Hunt*.

**PAUL WYETT**

DANNY

**Theatre** includes: *Sleepers Den* (Southwark Playhouse), *The Ballad of Yachiyo* (NT Studio/Gate), *Toast*, *My Heart's a Suitcase*, Young Writers' Festival 1991 and 1998 (Royal Court), *Dealer's Choice* (West Yorkshire Playhouse), *Billy Liar*, *Murmuring Judges*, *Arturo Ui*, *Bad Company*, *Fanta Babies*, *Price of Coal* (National & Studio), *Salt of the Earth* (Nottingham), *Space* (Soho Poly). **TV** includes: *Heartbeat*, *Pie in the Sky*, *Out of the Blue*, *Accused*, *Hang Gliding*, *First of the Summer Wine*. **Film:** *A Soldier's Tale*.

**SIMON BOWEN**

WRITER

As an actor his credits include appearances at the Bristol Old Vic, the National Theatre, on Radio 4, in film (*Fever Pitch*) and on TV *(The Secret Life of Michael Fry)*. He was encouraged to try his hand at writing by Bernard Kops. His association with Paines Plough began in 1999 when *Whitebaby* was performed at the Bristol Old Vic as part of *Western Front*. He joined their Wild Lunch writers' group in 2000, culminating in performance of a piece called *Waterloo. Free* is his first play.

**THEA SHARROCK**

DIRECTOR

Thea Sharrock is Artistic Director of Southwark Playhouse. She trained at the Anna Scher Theatre and the Market Theatre Johannesburg. Theatre includes *Top Girls* by Caryl Churchill (Oxford Stage Company national tour, Aldwych, second national tour for *Background*), *The Sleepers Den* by Peter Gill (Southwark Playhouse) and, as associate director, *Art* by Yasmina Reza (Wyndhams, Whitehall and touring). She received the James Menzies-Kitchin Memorial Trust's Young Director of the Year Award (2000) for which she first directed *Top Girls* at the BAC.

**RACHEL BLUES**

DESIGNER

Trained at Edinburgh College of Art and Bristol Old Vic Theatre School. Designs include: Top Girls (Oxford Stage Company, West End & UK tour), Silence, Winnie the Witch (Birmingham Rep), Belonging, The Sleepers Den (Southwark Playhouse), Loveplay (RSC), Ham (New Vic, Stoke), The Dove (Warehouse, Croydon), Bouncers (Bolton/Coventry), Car (Theatre Absolute/Coventry), Intimate Death (Gate, London). Two seasons at Oldham Coliseum. Currently working on Krindlekrax for Nottingham Playhouse & Birmingham Rep.

**PETE BULL**

LIGHTING DESIGNER

Pete Bull has lit shows as diverse as stand-up comedy and Greek tragedy, in venues ranging from upstairs in a pub to an open-air amphitheatre, in places as far apart as Vancouver and Clacton. He recently did the re-lights for the National's world tour of Hamlet, including a unique opportunity to light the show in Elsinore Castle.

**RICH WALSH**

SOUND DESIGNER

Work includes: The Walls (National), Exposure, Under The Blue Sky, On Raftery's Hill, Sacred Heart, Trust, Choice (Royal Court); 50 Revolutions (Whitehall); The Boy Who Left Home, The Nation's Favourite (UK tours), Yllana's 666 (Riverside Studios); Strike Gently Away From Body, Blavatsky (Young Vic Studio); Body And Soul, Soap Opera, The Baltimore Waltz (Upstairs At The Gatehouse), Small Craft Warnings (Pleasance); The Taming of the Shrew, Macbeth (Japanese tour); Dirk, Red Noses (Oxford Playhouse); The Wizard of Oz, The Winter's Tale (Old Fire Station, Oxford).

The Loft Theatre was created with the help of the Royal National Theatre Foundation.

Many of the projects in the *Transformation* season were developed in the National Theatre Studio.

*The Transformation* season is supported by Edward and Elissa Annunziato, Peter Wolff Theatre Trust, and by a gift from the estate of André Deutsch.

ON WORD graphics designed by typographer Alan Kitching using original wood letters.

The National's workshops are responsible for, on these productions: Armoury; Costume; Props & furniture; Scenic construction; Scenic painting; Wigs

NATIONAL THEATRE BOOKSHOP
The National's Bookshop in the Main Entrance foyer on the ground floor stocks a wide range of theatre-related books. Texts of all plays in the Loft during the Transformation season, and of the plays in *Channels (France)* are available from the NT Bookshop at £2.
T: 020 7452 3456; www.nationaltheatre.org.uk/bookshop

TRANSFORMATION SEASON TEAM
ARTISTIC ASSOCIATE Mick Gordon
ASSOCIATE PRODUCER Joseph Smith
ADMINISTRATOR Sarah Nicholson
LOFT THEATRE DESIGNER Will Bowen
FRONT OF HOUSE DESIGNER Jo Maund
FRONT OF HOUSE DESIGN PRODUCTION MANAGER Gavin Gibson
LITERARY MANAGER Jack Bradley
PLANNING PROJECT MANAGER Paul Jozefowski
RESIDENT DIRECTOR – LOFT Paul Miller
PRODUCTION CO-ORDINATOR Katrina Gilroy
PRODUCTION MANAGER – LOFT REALISATION Jo Maund
PRODUCTION ASSISTANTS – LOFT REALISATION Alan Bain, Gavin Gibson
LOFT LIGHTING REALISATION & TECHNICIANS Mike Atkinson, Steve Barnett,
Pete Bull, Huw Llewellyn, Cat Silver
LOFT SOUND REALISATION Adam Rudd, Rich Walsh
LOFT STAGE TECHNICIANS Danny O'Neill, Stuart Smith
MODEL MAKERS Aaron Marsden, Riette Hayes-Davies
GRAPHIC DESIGNERS Patrick Eley, Stephen Cummiskey
PROGRAMME EDITOR Dinah Wood
PRESS Lucinda Morrison, Mary Parker, Gemma Gibb
MARKETING David Hamilton-Peters
PRODUCTION PHOTOGRAPHER Sheila Burnett

*Thanks to the following people who were part of the original Lyttelton Development Group:* Ushi Bagga, Alice Dunne, Annie Eves-Boland, Jonathan Holloway, Gareth James, Mark Jonathan, Holly Kendrick, Paul Jozefowski, Angus MacKechnie, Tim Redfern, Chris Shutt, Matt Strevens, Jane Suffling, Nicola Wilson, Dinah Wood, Lucy Woollatt

# TRANSFORMATION SEASON

## IN THE LYTTELTON

A co-production between the National Theatre & Théâtre National de Chaillot

### The PowerBook . . . . . . . . . . . . . . . . . . . . . . . . . . . . . . . . . . . . . . . . . . 9 May–4 June
from a novel by Jeanette Winterson
devised by Jeanette Winterson, Deborah Warner & Fiona Shaw
Director Deborah Warner

### A Prayer for Owen Meany . . . . . . . . . . . . . . . . . . . . . . . . . . . . 10–29 June
a novel by John Irving
adapted by Simon Bent
Director Mick Gordon

A collaboration between the National Theatre & Trestle Theatre Company

### The Adventures of the Stoneheads . . . . . . . . . . . . . . . . . . . . . . 4–13 July
written & directed by Toby Wilsher

A collaboration between the National Theatre & Mamaloucos Circus

### The Birds . . . . . . . . . . . . . . . . . . . . . . . . . . . . . . . . . . . . . . . . . . . . . . 22 July–3 August
by Aristophanes, in a new version by Sean O'Brien
Director Kathryn Hunter

### Play Without Words . . . . . . . . . . . . . . . . . . . . . . . 20 August–14 September
devised & directed by Matthew Bourne

## IN THE LOFT

### Sing Yer Heart Out for the Lads . . . . . . . . . . . . . . . . . . 29 April–15 May
by Roy Williams
Director Simon Usher

### Free . . . . . . . . . . . . . . . . . . . . . . . . . . . . . . . . . . . . . . . . . . . . . . . . . . 20 May–8 June
by Simon Bowen
Director Thea Sharrock

### Life After Life . . . . . . . . . . . . . . . . . . . . . . . . . . . . . . . . . . . . . . . 28 May–8 June
a reportage play by Paul Jepson & Tony Parker
Director Paul Jepson

### The Shadow of a Boy . . . . . . . . . . . . . . . . . . . . . . . . . . . . . . . . . . 13–29 June
by Gary Owen
Director Erica Whyman

### The Mentalists . . . . . . . . . . . . . . . . . . . . . . . . . . . . . . . . . . . . . . . . 4–20 July
by Richard Bean
Director Sean Holmes

### Sanctuary . . . . . . . . . . . . . . . . . . . . . . . . . . . . . . . . . . . . 25 July–10 August
by Tanika Gupta
Director Hettie Macdonald

### The Associate . . . . . . . . . . . . . . . . . . . . . . . . . . . . . . . . . . . . . 15–31 August
by Simon Bent
Director Paul Miller

### Closing Time . . . . . . . . . . . . . . . . . . . . . . . . . . . . . . . . . . 4–21 September
by Owen McCafferty
Director James Kerr

# NATIONAL THEATRE STUDIO &
# TRANSFORMATION

All the plays in the LOFT are co-produced with the National Theatre Studio. The Studio is the National's laboratory for research and development, providing a workspace outside the confines of the rehearsal room and stage, where artists can experiment and develop their skills.

As part of its training for artists there is an on-going programme of classes, workshops, seminars, courses and masterclasses. Residencies have also been held in Edinburgh, Vilnius, Belfast and South Africa, enabling artists from a wider community to share and exchange experiences.

Central to the Studio's work is a commitment to new writing. The development and support of writers is demonstrated through play readings, workshops, short-term attachments, bursaries and sessions with senior writers. Work developed there continually reaches audiences throughout the country and overseas, on radio, film and television as well as at the National and other theatres. Most recent work includes the award-winning plays *Further than the Furthest Thing* by Zinnie Harris (Tron Theatre, Glasgow; Traverse, Edinburgh, and NT), *The Waiting Room* by Tanika Gupta (NT) and *Gagarin Way* by Gregory Burke (in association with Traverse, Edinburgh; NT; and at the Arts Theatre), *The Walls* by Colin Teevan (NT), *Accomplices* by Simon Bent, *Mr England* by Richard Bean (in association with Sheffield Theatres) and *The Slight Witch* by Paul Lucas (in association with Birmingham Rep), as well as a season of five new plays from around the world with the Gate Theatre, and *Missing Reel* by Toby Jones at the Traverse during the Edinburgh Festival 2001. *Gagarin Way* and *Further than the Furthest Thing* were part of SPRINGBOARDS – a series of partnerships created by the Royal National Theatre Studio with other theatres, enabling work by emerging writers to reach a wider audience.

Direct Action, a collaboration between The Studio and the Young Vic, is an initiative that provides young directors with an opportunity to work on the main stage of the Young Vic. Two plays were co-produced in the autumn of 2001: Max Frisch's *Andorra*, directed by Gregory Thompson; and David Rudkin's *Afore Night Come*, directed by Rufus Norris, who won the Evening Standard award for Best Newcomer for this production.

For the Royal National Theatre Studio

| | |
|---|---|
| HEAD OF STUDIO | Sue Higginson |
| STUDIO MANAGER | Matt Strevens |
| TECHNICAL MANAGER | Eddie Keogh |
| INTERNATIONAL PROJECTS MANAGER | Philippe Le Moine |
| RESIDENT DIRECTOR (LOFT) | Paul Miller |

Royal National Theatre
South Bank, London SE1 9PX
Box Office: 020 7452 3000
Information: 020 7452 3400

Registered Charity No: 224223

The chief aims of the National, under the direction of Trevor Nunn, are to present a diverse repertoire, embracing classic, new and neglected plays; to present these plays to the very highest standards; and to give audiences a wide choice.

All kinds of other events and services are on offer – short early-evening Platform performances; work for children and education work; free live entertainment both inside and outdoors at holiday times; exhibitions; live foyer music; backstage tours; bookshops; plenty of places to eat and drink; and easy car-parking. The nearby Studio acts as a resource for research and development for actors, writers and directors.

We send productions on tour, both in this country and abroad, and do all we can, through ticket-pricing, to make the NT accessible to everyone.

The National's home on the South Bank, opened in 1976, contains three separate theatres: the Olivier, the Lyttelton, and the Cottesloe and – during *Transformation* – a fourth: the Loft. It is open to the public all day, six days a week, fifty-two weeks a year. Stage by Stage – an exhibition on the NT's history, can be seen in the Olivier Gallery.

First published in 2002 by Oberon Books Ltd.
(incorporating Absolute Classics)
521 Caledonian Road, London N7 9RH
Tel: 020 7607 3637 / Fax: 020 7607 3629

e-mail: oberon.books@btinternet.com

A catalogue record for this book is available from the British
Library.

ISBN: 1 84002 300 7

Printed in Great Britain by Antony Rowe Ltd, Chippenham.

# Characters

KATE

SOPHIE

DANNY

DAVID

BEN

CHRIS

ALEX

NICK

## Note

The following script was correct at the time of going to press, but may differ slightly from the play as performed.

The symbol / is used in the text to indicate an interruption.

# Scene 1

*Reception area.*

*KATE stands by a desk. She waits. She picks up a phone. Dials.*

**Kate**  Hi. I think I spoke to you before. Yes. Hi. You were sending me a girl.

*SOPHIE enters.*

Okay. Hold it.

**Sophie**  Hi sorry.

**Kate**  I think we've got her now.

**Sophie**  Oh God.

**Kate**  No that's fine. Sorry.

**Sophie**  Is that the office.

**Kate**  No no problem. She wants a word.

*SOPHIE takes phone.*

**Sophie**  Sorry thanks. Hi sorry. No no it's fine everything's…sure. Okay. Thanks.

*KATE hangs up.*

**Kate**  Hi.

**Sophie**  Hi sorry.

**Kate**  Right. This is you for today.

**Sophie**  Okay.

**Kate**  You'll be welcoming clients

**Sophie**  Yes

**Kate**  Sending them through or asking them to wait. as appropriate.

**Sophie**  Right.

**Kate**  You'll need to lay out the magazines

**Sophie**  Okay.

**Kate**  Nicely on the table.

**Sophie**  Right.

**Kate**  I've done the post.

**Sophie**  Oh thanks have you sorry.

**Kate**  You should take any faxes to the person whose name is written on them.

*Beat.*

**Sophie**  Right.

**Kate**  There's a plan.

**Sophie**  Is there.

**Kate**  Yes. In the drawer. To tell you who's where

**Sophie**  In the office

**Kate**  Yes.

**Sophie**  Okay great

**Kate**  And answering the phone.

**Sophie**  (*Slight laugh.*) I've done that before.

**Kate**  (*Smiles.*) Have you.

**Sophie**  Yeah.

*Beat.*

Who's the big boss.

**Kate**  The big boss

**Sophie**  Yeah who's in charge. Just so I don't upset you know say fuck / or…

**Kate**  This is my company.

**Sophie**  Is it.

**Kate**  Yes.

**Sophie**  Oh right. Brilliant.

*Beat.*

Well done.

**Kate**  Thank you. Have you used this board before.

**Sophie**  Sorry?

**Kate**  This switchboard. have you –

**Sophie**  Uh I'm not sure

**Kate**  Well let's go through it

**Sophie**  …

**Kate**  Someone rings up okay

**Sophie**  …

**Kate**  You pick up the phone and find out who the caller is

**Sophie**  Yep

**Kate**  and who they want to speak to

**Sophie**  …yeah.

**Kate**  run down the names on the list…

**Sophie**  another? list in the drawer? Okay.

**Kate**  Across to their extension

**Sophie**  yes

**Kate**  hash button. punch the number. send. Okay.

*SOPHIE nods, smiles.*

Then you can just put the phone down. As normal. Alright? Any problems –

**Sophie**  Toilet.

**Kate**  Sorry.

**Sophie**  I need to know where the toilet is.

**Kate**  Right.

**Sophie**  For the clients. They might need to go.

**Kate**  Yes. Just around the corner.

**Sophie**  Fine.

*Beat.*

**Kate**  I think there might be something you're not saying.

**Sophie**  …

**Kate**  You look a little angry.

**Sophie**  Do I.

**Kate**  Yes.

**Sophie**  Oh. Oh dear…

**Kate**  Are you angry with me.

**Sophie**  (*Laughs.*) No. I'm really happy...happy to have got this day...the agency... I asked them to push me more towards more...creative type companies you know...better than the normal boring sort of...not that I mind, you know... I just need to get to some experience.

**Kate**  Because if you are angry you should say.

*Beat.*

**Sophie**  Really.

**Kate**  If any of my people are unhappy I need to know. I welcome and train every one of them personally. I want them to know who I am. I want them to talk to me. If we can't talk to each other how can we expect to do business.

*Beat.*

**Sophie**  I'm worth more than this.

**Kate**  (*Not sarcastic.*) Are you.

**Sophie**  I've got qualities. Good qualities.

**Kate**  Have you.

**Sophie**  Yes. But I don't fit an easy... I need to be interested in what I'm...

**Kate**  You need to be interested.

**Sophie**  I need to feel...

**Kate**  And you get angry. if you're not interested in what you're doing.

**Sophie**  Well...

**Kate**  Even if it's only for a day.

17

**Sophie**  I want something…concrete. I want something that will lead to something. I'm always moving about…there's no point in being good at anything or being nice…you never see the people again…nothing ever goes anywhere.

**Kate**  You don't want to be tied down.

**Sophie**  Well no…

**Kate**  You want to be flexible. You want to find the best possible situation for you.

**Sophie**  Yes exactly.

**Kate**  Until you find it you won't be –

**Sophie**  I'm not going to spend my life doing something I hate. And I've realised I've been allowing myself to be demanded of too much. I've put up with it. I want my demands…

**Kate**  Good.

**Sophie**  Yes.

**Kate**  So why are you angry.

**Sophie**  What.

**Kate**  Why do you hate me.

**Sophie**  I don't.

*Pause.*

**Kate**  Say some more.

**Sophie**  What?

**Kate**  Say some more.

**Sophie**  About what.

**Kate**  Anything we've been talking about. Anything else.

**Sophie**  …why.

**Kate**  It's important.

**Sophie**  Is it.

**Kate**  Yes say some / more.

**Sophie**  Oh for fuck's sake.

**Kate**  Good.

**Sophie**  Who the fuck do you think you are. Say some more.

**Kate**  You see you are angry.

**Sophie**  Look I came here to smile at suits and answer the phone and…get some experience so can I just…

**Kate**  I think you should own it.

**Sophie**  What.

**Kate**  I think you should own your anger.

**Sophie**  Jesus!

**Kate**  Say it: I am angry.

**Sophie**  So in control aren't you…

**Kate**  You're not angry with me.

**Sophie**  So bloody above it all.

**Kate**  You don't hate me.

**Sophie**  Don't I.

**Kate**  You should use your anger.

**Sophie**  Should I.

**Kate**  Your anger can push you.

**Sophie**  Can it.

**Kate**  Yes.

**Sophie**  Where.

**Kate**  Wherever you want to go.

**Sophie**  Really.

**Kate**  But you must own it and learn to use it. It can be destructive.

**Sophie**  Fine. Fuck you.

**Kate**  You're leaving.

**Sophie**  Yes. My anger. I'm using it to get me out of this…pisshole.

**Kate**  Good.

**Sophie**  Oh don't fucking –

**Kate**  What.

**Sophie**  Doesn't anything get to you. I was late. Now I'm leaving so –

**Kate**  I'll get someone else.

**Sophie**  From the agency.

**Kate**  Yes.

**Sophie**  Queueing up aren't they.

**Kate**  A lot of people just want to get some experience. In this field.

**Sophie**  God help them.

*SOPHIE exits. KATE dials.*

**Kate** Hi. I think I spoke to you. Yes. I need another girl.

*Phone rings.*

Just a minute. (*She changes line.*) Good morning –

*Beat.*

Oh hi. Yeah right. Look I'm kind of – it's a bit mad
here. Yes. Well I might be a while, I… Fine. Well we
could… Yes. We could meet up and…yes. We could do
something. Anything.

# Scene 2

*Train station waiting room.*

*DAVID and DANNY stand apart, facing each other.*

**Danny** And I say 'Don't worry mate, you'll get yours!' and
we cut. Don't worry mate, you'll get yours. If I get it of
course. Only a line but a big number. Big production I
mean. Big budget.

**David** A lot of money.

**Danny** (*Nods.*) TV.

**David** On television.

**Danny** Oh yeah network.

**David** Would that be good.

**Danny** God yeah loads of dosh.

**David** And for your career.

**Danny** The exposure.

**David**  Yes people might see you. Important people.

**Danny**  I doubt it.

**David**  I suppose they must be very busy.

**Danny**  Important people don't *watch* TV.

**David**  Don't they.

**Danny**  Too busy spending money off their faces. Jammy cunts. It's all about having a good face. If you haven't got a good face you're fucked. Nobody'll touch you.

**David**  I see.

**Danny**  Are you gorgeous? No. Are you an ugly bastard? No. Sorry. I'm an important person and you come to see me.

**David**  Right

**Danny**  Are you heavenly or a beast.

**David**  …

**Danny**  In that split second I first see you if I want to fuck you or beat you then I'm interested. I'll remember you. Otherwise…

**David**  You've got a good face.

**Danny**  No.

**David**  You have.

**Danny**  Please don't say that I shall get upset and it won't be pretty.

**David**  I'm sorry.

**Danny**  You apologised. How old-fashioned.

**David**  It was your face I noticed. Among. All the people.

**Danny**  My face is far too normal.

**David**  You looked…well –

**Danny**  I'm so normal I'm not even the boy next door.

**David**  I suppose you looked sad. Everybody pushing. Who were you waiting for.

**Danny**  I don't know. Someone.

**David**  Who.

**Danny**  I was waiting for you.

**David**  But you don't know me.

> *Beat.*
>
> Warm isn't it.
>
> *Beat.*

**Danny**  Take off your coat.

> *Beat.*
>
> If you're warm. You should take off your coat.
>
> *Beat.*
>
> Take off your coat.
>
> *Beat. DAVID takes off his coat. Beat.*
>
> What have you got. In your pocket.
>
> *Beat.*

**David**  Nothing.

**Danny**  You're a filthy liar.

*Beat.*

Do you want to know what I've got. In my pocket.

*Beat. DANNY puts his hand in his pocket.*

It's me. I've got me. In my pocket.

*We hear: 'Closing down closing down closing down closing down closing down. We're closing down this store. Elbow shove barge your way in ladies and gentlemen just to get at these bargains. Everything here today is a bargain and must be got rid of. We must be mad look at these prices we're giving it away ladies and gentlemen...'*

*DANNY produces a small tape recorder. Holds it up. Still running.*

Me. Did it for this shop. Bargain place. Opened up in town. Looped it. First thing they did was put this tape on. Ever since it opened it's been closing down. Been closing down for ages. Everything a bargain.

**David** Bastards.

**Danny** Easy peasy. Tourist trap.

*DANNY puts the tape recorder on the floor. They listen.*

**David** Must've. Given you a sore throat.

**Danny** No. I'm trained. I've got technique.

*Beat. Tape still running.*

**David** I'm not sure why I'm here.

**Danny** I'm not a whore.

**David** Why are you here.

**Danny**  I crave new experience. If I didn't do something different every day…well… I don't know what I'd do. How long have you got.

**David**  Not long. Couple of hours.

**Danny**  Oh ages.

**David**  I must be mad.

**Danny**  So what shall we do.

**David**  You could be anybody.

**Danny**  Anybody could be anybody. Nowadays.

*Beat.*

We should do something.

**David**  Where are you from.

**Danny**  Yawn yawn boring boring.

**David**  I mean originally.

**Danny**  Do you like my shoes.

**David**  I mean your accent.

**Danny**  Aren't they shiny.

**David**  Your voice. Doesn't sound like.

**Danny**  Would you like me to walk on you

**David**  Doesn't sound like you're from / round here.

**Danny**  Is that what you want. You want me to walk all over you.

**David**  Look.

**Danny**  I'm going to stand on your face.

**David**  Look stop it.

**Danny**  I'm going to shit in your mouth. That's what you want isn't it.

**David**  Can you just stop

**Danny**  You want to be nothing. Do you. You want to be the maggot in the shit ground into the stinking fucking floor. Do you.

**David**  Please

**Danny**  You've come to the right place.

**David**  Look…

**Danny**  You have arrived. You're here. Now get on your knees and admit it. I am shit. I want to be shit.

*Pause.*

**David**  I think I should go.

**Danny**  What.

**David**  I'm going to go.

**Danny**  Like fuck.

**David**  Yes I'm –

**Danny**  Give me something.

**David**  What.

**Danny**  Something for my trouble.

**David**  You mean money. You want some money.

**Danny**  Are you the law. I'll fucking kill you. I'm not a tart.

*DANNY looks around. DAVID finds wallet.*

You got a camera in here. Eh?

**David**  No. Look here's –

**Danny**  Don't give me money you cunt (*Shouts to unseen camera.*) I am not a whore.

*Beat.*

**David**  Look I arrived this morning. I'm not a policeman. I'm nobody. I'm just a… I'm retired I… (*Breaking.*) …I don't know why I'm here.

*Beat.*

**Danny**  I want some shiny trousers.

**David**  …what.

**Danny**  Some expensive shiny trousers. Party trousers. I need them.

**David**  Take some fucking – there some fucking money – take it alright. Take it. Go on. Now fuck off and leave me alone.

*DANNY picks up notes. Picks up tape recorder. Stops it.*

**Danny**  Temper temper.

*DANNY exits as BEN enters. BEN waits. Tries not to look at DAVID who is collecting himself. DAVID struggles to put his coat on. Catches BEN looking at him. They look at each other for a moment as CHRIS enters.*

**Chris**  Where is it.

**Ben**  …Hi.

**Chris**  Your bag. Where's your pack.

*DAVID exits. Beat.*

**Ben**  My rucksack.

**Chris**  Where is it.

**Ben**  Chris

**Chris**  What.

**Ben**  I'm not going

**Chris**  …You're not coming.

**Ben**  I'm not coming

**Chris**  …You're staying

**Ben**  I've changed my mind

**Chris**  …You're not coming

**Ben**  …No. No I'm not.

**Chris**  Right.

   *Beat.*

   Prick.

**Ben**  Sorry

**Chris**  Sorry.

**Ben**  It's okay

**Chris**  Prick.

   *Beat.*

   Why. Why not.

   *Beat.*

**Ben**  Well. Look. I just. I just want to stay

**Chris**  You want to stay. Here

**Ben**  Yeah

**Chris**  Right I see

**Ben**  No listen. I think I feel

**Chris**  You've got a ticket to go halfway round the world.

**Ben**  I've been halfway round the world.

**Chris**  Not this way.

*Beat.*

**Ben**  I actually feel quite good. Just. Working.

**Chris**  Do you.

**Ben**  Yeah. My job. I'm doing well. I think. I like it. I think I'm quite good at it.

**Chris**  Really.

**Ben**  I feel like

**Chris**  …

**Ben**  You'll laugh.

**Chris**  I'm fit to fucking piss myself.

*Beat.*

**Ben**  I'm sorry

**Chris**  Oh fuck off.

**Ben**  I am.

*Beat.*

I feel like. In a small way. Perhaps I'm stupid. I don't know. I feel like I'm starting to get somewhere.

**Chris**  Where.

**Ben**  You know what I mean.

**Chris**  …Do I.

*Beat.*

**Ben**  Look. When are we going to stop. I mean. What are
we going to do. Really. What are we going to do.

**Chris**  We're going to fuck off on a plane halfway round
the world we're going to see some amazing places meet
interesting people we're going to get off our faces and
we're going to spend all the money we've eaten shit to
earn for the last however long. And when we've done
that we're going to

**Ben**  We're going to make another load of cash and fuck off
and do it all over again.

**Chris**  Maybe

**Ben**  Yeah. Maybe.

*Beat.*

**Chris**  Well. If you want to give up.

**Ben**  Give up.

**Chris**  If you want to slow down. Stop.

**Ben**  I want something to stay the same. I want to know
where I am.

**Chris**  For how long.

**Ben**  I don't know. For a while. What.

**Chris**  Nothing.

**Ben**  No come on. Don't smile like that and say nothing. What are you thinking. Say it for fuck's sake.

**Chris**  For a while. Just for a while. That's what everyone says. A while. I'll just do it for a while. Bollocks. You're getting sucked in.

**Ben**  It's not like that. Sucked in to what.

**Chris**  I knew you'd do this. I fucking knew it.

**Ben**  I knew you'd be like this.

**Chris**  Like what.

**Ben**  Like this. Angry.

**Chris**  Why shouldn't I be fucking angry we're supposed to be going off again we've planned this for fucking ages and you turn up on the morning we're going and say you're not going. What am I supposed to do.

**Ben**  Understand?

*Beat.*

**Chris**  Oh I understand.

**Ben**  Do you.

**Chris**  Oh yeah.

**Ben**  Really.

**Chris**  Yeah. You're insecure. You need approval. You're bright. But you're. Weak. You need something else. Something. I don't know. Something to tell you you're worth something.

**Ben**  And that's a crime.

**Chris**  You're nearly brilliant. Nearly.

**Ben**  Thanks

**Chris**  But you're not. And I don't know if you will be.

**Ben**  Don't you

**Chris**  No. Not after today.

*Beat.*

**Ben**  Well thanks. Thanks very much.

*Beat.*

I've got a meeting. This morning. With the guy. The guy who runs the company. He wants to see me. I think I've been doing. Really well. Lately. He wants to see me. He's expanding. I'm. I'm excited. I am. Maybe I'm being stupid. But. I feel. Positive.

**Chris**  Do you.

**Ben**  Yes.

**Chris**  That's good.

**Ben**  Yes. It is.

**Chris**  A positive worker is a good worker. Isn't it Benjamin.

*BEN looks at CHRIS.*

**Ben**  You don't understand anything.

**Chris**  Don't I.

**Ben**  You're scared. Aren't you. You don't want to go on your own. You never want to do anything on your own. You can't. You always act like I'm frustrating you. Or somehow not as relaxed. Or open as you are. But you need me. You think you're such an individual. But going on your own. Terrifies you. Doesn't it.

**Chris** No.

*Beat.*

**Ben** I'm your best mate.

**Chris** Best mate from travelling.

**Ben** I think I know what you're like. Your problem is. You're moody. You don't want to fit in with anybody. You don't want to find anything. Or find somewhere to be. You're not going away looking for anything. You're just going away. And you'll always be going away cos you can't take any responsibility. For anything. Because you're selfish. Because you're weak. Because you're a fucking child. Actually.

*Pause.*

I just want to know where I am. For a while. I like the company. I think. I think I'm starting to like myself. A bit more. Which means I like it here. Funny. It's big and it's dirty. I know. But I want to stay. I want to. It feels right.

*Beat.*

I'm sorry I got carried away

**Chris** No no

**Ben** I was out of order

**Chris** You didn't mean it then.

*Beat.*

**Ben** Did you mean what you said.

*Beat.*

**Chris** Go.

**Ben**  Christ why is this so intense it's like we're fucking married or something.

**Chris**  Who'd marry you.

**Ben**  Who'd marry you.

*Beat.*

I want to laugh. But

**Chris**  Go on fuck off.

**Ben**  That's what you're doing. Isn't it.

**Chris**  Maybe. Go on. Go. You'll be late for your meeting.

*They look at each other for a moment or two. BEN exits.*

# Scene 3

*Restaurant lobby.*

*ALEX waiting. SOPHIE enters with a barely concealed can of lager.*

**Sophie**  Sorry

**Alex**  I've been trying to get you.

**Sophie**  Yeah it's off.

**Alex**  Why.

**Sophie**  I just…it's nice not to be contacted sometimes. Okay.

**Alex**  You finish early.

**Sophie**  I walked out.

**Alex**  …you walked out.

**Sophie**  Yeah I…yeah.

**Alex**  What happened.

**Sophie**  Just…the woman…she

**Alex**  What.

**Sophie**  She was just… I don't know. we didn't get on.

**Alex**  You didn't get on so you walked out.

**Sophie**  No. we had an argument. (*Swigs.*)

**Alex**  Look sit down have a

*He indicates vodka, ice, mixer on table.*

**Sophie**  Are we getting a table.

**Alex**  Thirty to forty minutes.

**Sophie**  Didn't you phone up and reserve –

**Alex**  Look I'm sorry I forgot it was crazy today okay.

*Beat. SOPHIE sits.*

So what did you do.

**Sophie**  Today… Do you know I had the best day…
Probably the best day I've had for…well…ages.

**Alex**  Oh yeah.

**Sophie**  Yeah I just went off and…got lost.

**Alex**  Lost. Lost where.

**Sophie**  I don't know…all over the place… Christ knows
where I ended up.

**Alex**  You want to be careful.

**Sophie**  Oh Alex for God's sake

**Alex**  I'm serious you're too…trusting.

**Sophie**  And you're a sensible bloody…

**Alex**  No I'm not.

*Beat.*

**Sophie**  You know this city. It's. Beautiful.

*ALEX snorts.*

It is. When you've got a bit of time. When you can just look. I mean stop and look. And. See. You know.

**Alex**  See what.

**Sophie**  Everything that's there. Everything you miss because you're running around like a fucking maniac

**Alex**  Like what.

**Sophie**  …what.

**Alex**  Everything you miss like what.

**Sophie**  Like…like okay. Like today I was just walking about whatever and I don't know when but I just. Suddenly I just saw the buildings. Above the shops. I mean I go in out of these places how fucking often I don't know but above them. Are all these other buildings. Fantastic some of them.

**Alex**  Offices.

**Sophie**  Yeah yeah…whatever.

*Beat.*

It's a really. Really. Shite example. But. Know what I mean.

**Alex**  (*Looks at bags.*) So you went shopping.

*SOPHIE has finished her can. She pours herself a drink.*

**Sophie**  Yeah couple of things.

**Alex**  A couple.

**Sophie**  I'd just had such a. Brilliant day. Hadn't really done anything but. it felt so good. And I thought, 'Don't feel guilty.' Why give yourself such a hard time all the time. Get yourself something. Go on. You deserve it. You're a nice person. Buy yourself a present.

**Alex**  Credit card.

**Sophie**  Yeah

**Alex**  Never-never land.

**Sophie**  Just thought fuck it you know. They were fine. I phoned them.

*SOPHIE swigs at her drink. Beat.*

What. What is it.

**Alex**  Nothing.

**Sophie**  You've gone in a mood what is it.

**Alex**  Well –

**Sophie**  Come on.

**Alex**  Well. Today you've managed to lose a day's pay then wander round spending money you haven't got on things you probably don't need.

**Sophie**  …

**Alex**  I just. Sometimes

**Sophie**  What. Sometimes what.

**Alex**  Who's going to have to bail you out / when you're short

**Sophie**  You won't have to bail me out.

**Alex**  No.

**Sophie**  I earn my own money.

**Alex**  I don't mind helping you out.

**Sophie**  Twice. Twice you have lent me a hundred pounds and both times I have paid you back.

**Alex**  No your sister –

**Sophie**  Yeah and you took it didn't you.

**Alex**  Oh so I should –

**Sophie**  No. No I'm sorry.

*Pause.*

Let's go away.

**Alex**  Sophie

**Sophie**  Just a couple of days. I don't care.

**Alex**  We will alright we will. When I get a minute to… I'm tired.

*Beat.*

**Sophie**  Busy today. Silly question.

**Alex**  Yeah.

**Sophie**  You eaten.

**Alex**  Sandwich from the sandwich man.

*SOPHIE smiles. Beat.*

Sometimes I think

**Sophie**  What.

**Alex**  Sometimes I just want to…

**Sophie**  What.

**Alex**  … (*Nondescript gesture.*)

**Sophie**  …what. Sometimes you just want to – (*Copies, craply.*)

**Alex**  Yeah. And then I want to just…throw it all away.

**Sophie**  Yeah.

**Alex**  Yep.

**Sophie**  You mean that.

**Alex**  Wrap it all up in a big ball of shite and ram it back up God's arse.

*SOPHIE is giggling.*

**Sophie**  What?

**Alex**  What.

**Sophie**  What!

**Alex**  Everything.

**Sophie**  Work everything.

**Alex**  Work everything life everything me me everything…

*Gigglebeat.*

**Sophie**  How is it. work.

**Alex**  Brilliant. Surpassing all forecasts. Breaking all records. Shite.

**Sophie**  Crying all the way to the bank.

**Alex**  Oh yes.

*Beat.*

Where is this fucking table.

**Sophie** Sorry

*ALEX smiles. NICK appears holding a carrier bag.*

**Nick** Excuse me. I think you left this in the toilet.

**Alex** Oh – Christ.

**Nick** I've been trying to find you…

**Alex** That's so good of you.

**Nick** Not at all. These things aren't cheap.

**Sophie** What is it.

**Nick** Latest Dreamcast type…

*NICK produces it.*

**Sophie** …?

**Nick** It's like a game. Boys' thing.

**Sophie** Been shopping.

**Alex** No no, (*To NICK.*) I had the best figures last month. in the office. you can choose like a prize or whatever.

**Nick** Good idea. Incentives. Fun.

**Sophie** What were the other things

**Alex** Oh…um there was gift vouchers. you know. hamper, weekend away –

**Sophie** What.

**Alex** …A weekend away.

**Sophie** …For two.

**Alex**  Yeah.

**Sophie**  Where.

**Alex**  Oh I don't know somewhere nice I imagine. Swanky hotel. You know.

**Sophie**  And you chose this.

**Alex**  …Yeah I…yeah.

**Sophie**  Great.

**Nick**  So that'll be you for the next…

**Alex**  Oh God.

**Nick**  Glued to the set.

**Alex**  Addictive.

**Nick**  Once you get on it…

*Beat.*

**Alex**  Listen I know you don't I

**Nick**  That's funny but I was going to say

**Alex**  That party

**Nick**  Oh God

**Alex**  Yes

**Nick**  Oh God. You're a friend of Ben's

**Alex**  From back home. Yes. Haven't spoken for a while.

**Nick**  Hi.

**Alex**  Hi. God!

*SOPHIE is waiting. ALEX senses suddenly.*

Sorry this is Sophie.

**Sophie**  Hello.

**Nick**  Nick. Hi. (*Points.*) Alex…?

**Alex**  Yes. That party.

**Nick**  Oh Christ.

**Alex**  How faced were we.

**Nick**  Oh Christ.

*SOPHIE has finished her drink; starts on ALEX's.*

**Alex**  What was it for that party. I mean –

**Nick**  I'm afraid I really don't remember.

**Alex**  Did you come to –

**Sophie**  I don't know.

**Alex**  I don't think you did.

*Beat.*

**Nick**  Right anyway.

**Alex**  Look join us.

**Sophie**  Alex

**Nick**  No I couldn't.

**Alex**  What.

**Sophie**  Nothing. Look

**Nick**  No.

**Alex**  Come on come on have a drink we're waiting for a table. Have you had the sea bass here.

**Nick**  I must confess I haven't.

**Sophie**  Alex

**Alex**  Right that settles it.

*ALEX pulls out chair.*

I'm giving you an order.

**Nick**  Really.

**Sophie**  Alex.

**Nick**  I shouldn't.

**Alex**  Sit – ah ah ah sit! I will not allow you to live another night in this city not knowing the exquisite pleasure of the aforementioned fish dish.

**Nick**  Well. Alright then.

*NICK sits. SOPHIE stands.*

**Sophie**  I'm going to go

**Alex**  What.

**Sophie**  Yeah. I'm not so

*ALEX takes SOPHIE aside.*

**Alex**  What are you doing.

**Sophie**  I'm going home

**Alex**  You're in a mood

**Sophie**  No

**Alex**  For fuck's sake

**Sophie**  No. It's fine.

**Alex**  Sophie come on

**Sophie**  Come on?

**Alex**  …What.

**Sophie**  Let's go away. We will. I'm tired. We could've. But no. No. You choose some. Game box.

**Alex**  …

**Sophie**  And now you invite some lunatic I've never met to eat with us. Just when we really need an evening. An evening just…

**Alex**  Maybe you do.

**Sophie**  …Oh. Fine.

**Alex**  I think…maybe we need…

**Nick**  Look maybe I should –

**Alex**  Sit down please. Nick please just sit down.

*NICK pours himself a drink.*

(*With SOPHIE again.*) I think we need to socialise more. Have some fun.

**Sophie**  And an evening with me / wouldn't be fun.

**Alex**  No look you know what I mean

**Sophie**  Fine that's fine. I'm glad you said that. Now I really am going.

**Alex**  You're going

**Sophie**  Yeah

**Alex**  …okay

**Sophie**  Okay. Fine.

**Alex**  …Okay.

*Beat.*

**Sophie**  Goodbye Nick. Enjoy your dinner. (*Exits.*)

**Nick**  Everything okay.

**Alex**  Yeah yeah no problem. Drink up.

# Scene 4

*A small gallery.*

*DAVID and KATE looking at pictures.*

**David**  Brilliant. God. Amazing isn't it. Look at that picture. So clever.

*KATE has moved on to the next, gives it a glance and again moves on.*

Didn't have the cameras we've got. Like bloody black boxes. Not like now. Make you a bloody dinner. Seen this.

**Kate**  Yeah.

**David**  Messed about in the darkroom. That's how he did it.

**Kate**  …Yeah?

**David**  Used all sorts of tricks. When he was developing.

**Kate**  Oh.

*KATE looks at watch.*

**David**  What's the rush.

**Kate**  Nothing.

**David**  (*Joking.*) You big city people. You want to slow down.

**Kate**  I don't think we have very long.

**David**  They won't mind.

**Kate**  I'm sure the people here have homes to go to.

**David**  Well a couple of minutes won't hurt. Honestly. What's it come to if people can't relax the rules a bit.

**Kate**  I'm sure it's nothing personal.

**David**  Anyway I was here in plenty of time.

**Kate**  You should have come in.

**David**  Don't be daft.

**Kate**  I told you I might be late.

**David**  No point in going round on my own. Come all this way.

**Kate**  I didn't know you were coming. I was working. I had to sort out a problem.

**David**  Thought you'd have a little man to do that for you.

**Kate**  No. I handle everything.

**David**  Do you.

**Kate**  Yes. Yes I do.

**David**  Oh. well done.

*Pause. An announcement: 'Ladies and Gentlemen we will be closing in two minutes. You have two minutes ladies and gentlemen. Thank you.' They look at each other.*

So you must come here. Do you.

**Kate**  What.

**David**  This place. Expect you come here quite a bit.

**Kate**  You sound like you're trying to get my phone number.

*Beat.*

No. Not really.

**David**  What. Great place like this.

**Kate**  I don't actually get out that much.

**David**  Good God all the shows they have.

**Kate**  Well. I work quite hard and…

**David**  Nothing like this back home.

**Kate**  Sometimes you just forget what's going on.

**David**  Forget!

**Kate**  There is quite a lot happening down here.

**David**  Oh is there.

**Kate**  Yes and you're a bit spoilt. Spoilt for choice.

**David**  Oh.

**Kate**  Because you have so many things happening. Well.

**David**  What.

**Kate**  You don't appreciate it.

**David**  Bloody madness.

**Kate**  You don't have time to see them all.

**David**  Honestly.

**Kate**  You get used to missing things. You have to. So many cool things going on.

**David**  Cool.

**Kate**  You have to let go a bit. Realise you can't do everything.

**David**  Can't do nothing though can you.

**Kate**  What like back home.

*Beat.*

I don't do nothing.

**David**  What do you do then.

**Kate**  You know what I do I –

**David**  I know you live down here I know you work down here but I don't really know what you do.

**Kate**  …

**David**  You don't call. Do you. So no. I don't know what you do.

**Kate**  Look.

**David**  Not really. not day to day.

**Kate**  Let's not have a scene.

**David**  What do you do.

*Beat.*

**Kate**  Dad. I do want to talk about this. I do. But can we not talk about it here. Not now.

*Beat. DAVID studies a picture.*

**David**  See that.

48

**Kate** …?

**David** Look. He's. The way he's made the line of that woman's body. It's like a line see. Soft focus on the body. All dark around the outside.

*KATE checks watch, finds mobile.*

**Kate** (*To DAVID.*) …?

**David** Like a shadow. Like a cut-out person or –

*KATE is dialling.*

He was famous for that.

**Kate** (*Phone.*) Hi. Rachel. It's me. Hi. Everything okay. Good.

**David** Very famous. In his day.

**Kate** Just wanted to make sure.

**David** Still well-known now. Well. (*Gestures at exhibition.*)

**Kate** So that's you. Nearly finished.

**David** Everybody's still talking about him. For taking a few pictures.

**Kate** (*Slight laugh.*) Now you've learnt the ropes you're leaving us.

**David** Even though he's dead. Dead and gone for years.

**Kate** Yes your first day was your last day. (*Slight laugh.*)

**David** Perhaps because he's dead. Everyone talking about him.

**Kate** Well. Thank you. Very much. Yes.

*An announcement: 'Ladies and gentlemen we are now closed. We are now closed. Thank you.'*

Oh. I think we're about to be thrown out.

**David**  Famous famous man.

**Kate**  No. Looks a bit cold out there.

**David**  The famous camera man.

**Kate**  Yes the usual girl will be back tomorrow.

**David**  We all talk about him because he's dead.

**Kate**  Yes. Thank you. Goodbye.

*KATE hangs up. Thinks.*

# Scene 5

*Cocktail bar.*

*ALEX and NICK stand by a rail that holds their glasses. They can lean but not sit.*

**Nick**  Are we empty.

*ALEX struggles to look at glasses, looks back at NICK slowly.*

So.

**Alex**  What.

**Nick**  Is there anything left. In our 'tumblers'.

**Alex**  Do you know. I don't know.

**Nick**  You just looked.

**Alex**  Yes.

**Nick**  What was there.

**Alex**  I don't remember.

**Nick**  Tell me the truth. Can you no longer see.

**Alex**  Yes. I can see. But it's dark in here.

**Nick**  It is not dark in here, it is (*With some effort.*) subtly lit.

*They laugh. NICK raises glass.*

André.

**Alex**  Yes. André. Who is he.

**Nick**  Head man here. Behind the bar.

**Alex**  Head bar man.

**Nick**  Exactly.

**Alex**  You know him.

**Nick**  No.

**Alex**  Makes a fucking fine spring punch.

**Nick**  Exactly.

**Alex**  Finest spring punch I've ever had.

**Nick**  Moreish.

**Alex**  Mmm.

*ALEX lifts glass.*

**Nick**  From Europe.

**Alex**  Yes.

**Nick**  André.

**Alex**  Ah. Where. In Europe.

**Nick**  I don't fucking know.

**Alex**  Oh.

**Nick**  And I don't fucking care.

*They laugh.*

Fuck him.

**Alex**  Yes.

**Nick**  Fuck André and his fucking fine spring punch.

**Alex**  (*USA.*) Fuck him inne ass.

*Laughter.*

**Nick**  Fucking Europeans.

**Alex**  Come over here.

**Nick**  Drink our women.

*Laughter.*

**Alex**  Fuck em.

**Nick**  Fuck em all.

*Clink glasses. Drink.*

**Alex**  Empty.

**Nick**  Mmm.

**Alex**  Air punch.

**Nick**  (*Giggle.*) Mmm.

**Alex**  Saucy little number.

*Beat.*

**Nick**  What shall we do.

**Alex**  Now.

**Nick**  Yes.

**Alex**  Well. I'm alright. Are you.

**Nick**  Yes. I think I am.

**Alex**  I have money.

**Nick**  How much.

**Alex**  Quite enough. Do you have money.

**Nick**  You know I do.

**Alex**  Yeah you've got fucking loads haven't you.

**Nick**  Yes. Yes I have.

**Alex**  Well then we can do…

**Nick**  I am post-economic.

**Alex**  My God are you really.

**Nick**  Yes.

**Alex**  …Excellent.

**Nick**  Yes.

**Alex**  How does that work then.

**Nick**  What.

**Alex**  …Being…like that.

**Nick**  I do not need to work now. Nor will I ever need to again.

**Alex**  Oh.

**Nick**  I shall retire at thirty-five.

**Alex**  Really.

**Nick**  Or thereabouts.

**Alex**  I see. So what do you –

**Nick**  I oversee my company.

**Alex**  Oh.

**Nick**  It will be sold to someone bigger within the next five years.

**Alex**  Will it.

**Nick**  Yes. I am expecting seven figures.

**Alex**  Really.

**Nick**  Possibly eight.

**Alex**  Eight figures. Christ.

*Beat.*

How is Ben.

**Nick**  Fine.

**Alex**  Really.

**Nick**  He's doing very well.

**Alex**  Good.

**Nick**  What do you do again.

**Alex**  Recruitment. Financial and –

**Nick**  You're a head-hunter aren't you.

**Alex**  Yes.

**Nick**  Is it enough.

**Alex**  I'm sorry.

**Nick**  Are you a happy head-hunter.

**Alex**  Well

**Nick**  No then.

**Alex**  Not really.

**Nick**  Come to Cambridge.

**Alex**  …?

**Nick**  I'm relocating. Come and work for me.

**Alex**  In Cambridge.

**Nick**  It's exploding. Start-ups. Silicon. Going sky-high.
  Mental.

**Alex**  Is it.

**Nick**  I've realised I need someone.

**Alex**  Do you.

**Nick**  In Human Resources. I need someone.

**Alex**  What for.

**Nick**  To find very bright people. People who have an urge
  to make something happen in the world.

**Alex**  I see.

**Nick**  Hey. HEY YOU.

*DANNY approaches.*

Give me a punch.

**Danny**  Can I have that in writing.

**Nick**  And him too.

**Danny**  Haven't you boys had enough.

**Nick**  Of course that's why we want some more.

**Danny**  Ice.

**Nick**  Please.

*As DANNY exits.*

**Alex**  Seems like a nice boy.

*They roar.*

**Nick**  What about your…lady.

**Alex**  Sophie.

**Nick**  Is that her name.

**Alex**  What about her.

**Nick**  Well I mean…

**Alex**  It's a funny time. We've been… I'm not sure we know where we are. I don't know if we both need to be clearer. On our direction. I mean individually. Before we can…

**Nick**  Some things lead to other things. Life is about choices.

**Alex**  …Yeah.

**Nick**  I need someone. Someone who really knows / people.

**Alex**  I know people

**Nick**  How they work.

**Alex**  Yes

**Nick**  How to root them out.

**Alex**  Yes. Get leads

**Nick**  How to get them.

**Alex**  How to close them

**Nick**  Yes. How to keep them. The good people.

**Alex**  I might be expensive.

*Beat. They both roar.*

**Nick**  Where is my drink.

**Alex**  Shame they don't have a screen in here

**Nick**  You want to watch football.

**Alex**  Plug in the dream machine

**Nick**  Amazing graphics

**Alex**  Got the kung fu game and the racing. The driving one with

**Nick**  You wouldn't want to play with me.

**Alex**  Oh wouldn't I

**Nick**  I'd whip your ass boy

**Alex**  Oh yeah

**Nick**  Oh yes indeed

**Alex**  Not if I whipped yours first. Sweetheart.

*They roar. DANNY enters. Waits.*

Are you going to give me my drink.

**Danny**  Are you going to give me my money.

**Nick**  No. I am going pay you some cash. And you are going to do your fucking job.

*NICK finds money. He holds it out, then drops it; accidentally on purpose.*

Oops.

*NICK and ALEX snigger. Pause. DANNY bends to the floor, picks up the money, puts the drinks down on the floor.*

**Danny** Enjoy. (*He exits.*)

**Nick** Cunt.

*ALEX kneels and gets his drink. Stays there.*

**Alex** Ah…

*NICK looks down at him.*

**Nick** Are you having a piss.

**Alex** Not that I know of.

**Nick** Then what are you doing.

**Alex** I'm just. Taking it easy.

**Nick** I have to say mate. You are on the fucking floor.

*They both laugh.*

**Alex** I am. Aren't I.

*Both still laughing. ALEX puts down his drink cack-handedly.*

Oops.

**Nick** Actually

**Alex** What…

**Nick** That's something I haven't done for fucking ages.

**Alex** What.

**Nick** Slam.

**Alex**  I am not dancing with you Nicholas.

**Nick**  No no no. You stupid. Fucking. Kneeler.

*They laugh. NICK struggles to the floor, takes his drink.*

**Alex**  Oh… Slamming…how old are you…

**Nick**  Fuck. Off.

**Alex**  Can you slam spring punch.

*NICK slams. Drinks. Swallows. Beat.*

**Nick**  Oh I think so. (*Goes for ALEX's drink.*) Shall I show you –

*ALEX evades his grasp.*

**Alex**  I think I can remember.

**Nick**  Are you positive.

**Alex**  Absolutely.

*ALEX holds glass on the floor.*

You know. You forgot one very vital. Thing.

**Nick**  (*Stunned.*) Did I.

**Alex**  The count.

**Nick**  Oh!?

**Alex**  See… (*Holding glass.*) …one…two…two and a half…
two and three quarters…two and seven-eighths…two
and seven eighths and a lil biddy bit…

**Nick**  Oh just fucking do it will you.

*NICK grabs ALEX's arm and makes him slam the drink,
too hard. The glass smashes.*

Ooops.

*NICK laughs, as ALEX looks at the drink on the floor, the smashed glass in his hand. NICK rolls, ALEX looks at him, giggles, then looks back at his hand.*

**Alex**  …? Ow…

*NICK screams with laughter.*

**Nick**  (*Helpless.*) …Ow!

*ALEX giggles. His hand is bleeding.*

# Scene 6

*Airport.*

*CHRIS is sitting. SOPHIE strides in.*

**Sophie**  Excuse me… Where is customer services.

**Chris**  Huh.

**Sophie**  I said…fuck does nobody know –

**Chris**  Hang on

**Sophie**  I just want to complain and nobody seems to know where I should go.

**Chris**  What is it.

**Sophie**  I fell asleep on the tube on the way home only had a zone two. Ended up here they charge me excess.

**Chris**  This is the airport.

**Sophie**  Wouldn't take my word for it.

**Chris**  I'm waiting for a plane.

**Sophie**  Why will nobody listen to. An honest explanation I mean.

**Chris**  What do you want me to do about it.

*Beat.*

Look.

**Sophie**  What.

**Chris**  Look at that.

**Sophie**  The aeroplane.

**Chris**  Jesus. Look.

**Sophie**  Yes. It's taking off.

**Chris**  Watch.

**Sophie**  …

**Chris**  Look at it. The power. And you know that everyone on board is sweating. Tense and not talking. Or smiling and talking too much. Panicking. Everybody. And from here. Just a little distance…it looks so smooth.

*Beat.*

Every time I see a plane I have to stop. I have to wait. 'Til it's flown over. Out of sight. And I have to watch it. I have to. It's like…if I don't watch it maybe something'll happen…if I don't keep my eyes on this big machine full of people. It might fall out of the sky. I have to concentrate.

And yet. All the time I'm watching it. It feels like it's going to happen anyway. Like I can't do anything. Like there is no way this thing can stay in the air. It is going to crash. It is.

I'm always amazed when an aeroplane doesn't fall out of the sky. I must've watched thousands. I've seen thousands fly by. Land safely. I've never seen one crash. Not really. Not with my own eyes. Yet I still think that is what's going to happen. Why is that. My experience is telling me something but I will not allow it. My brain or my body – or…just me… I still feel it. That fear.

*Beat.*

But then I'm a weirdo.

*SOPHIE laughs. Beat.*

**Sophie**  Travelling.

**Chris**  Got a hopper. Going East.

**Sophie**  Nice.

**Chris**  Nice?

**Sophie**  Yeah. To…be travelling. You going by yourself.

**Chris**  …Yeah.

**Sophie**  …wow.

**Chris**  Someone else was supposed to. Be coming along but

**Sophie**  Oh.

**Chris**  They didn't…they decided not to.

**Sophie**  Right.

*Beat.*

**Chris**  Why would you turn down an opportunity like that.

**Sophie**  Like…

**Chris**  To just. Take off.

**Sophie**  …I don't know.

**Chris**  Neither do I.

**Sophie**  I suppose. They must have had their reasons.

**Chris**  What reasons are there. To stay in this city any longer than you have to.

*Beat.*

**Sophie**  Well.

*Beat.*

I don't know.

**Chris**  He had reasons.

**Sophie**  He. He did.

**Chris**  Not good ones. But he had reasons. (*Smiles.*) Mates.

*SOPHIE smiles nervously.*

**Sophie**  Will you… I mean. Will you be okay.

**Chris**  Yeah. Course.

**Sophie**  You won't have anyone to –

**Chris**  To what.

**Sophie**  …I don't know.

**Chris**  I'll be fine.

*Pause.*

**Sophie**  I'm so pissed off. Ten fucking quid they charged me. And I'm skint.

**Chris**  (*Shopping bags.*) Don't look skint.

**Sophie**  That's *why* I'm skint.

**Chris**  Don't stress.

**Sophie**  Oh right. Don't stress.

**Chris**  I'm serious. You have to accept being broke. Don't fight it. If you fight it you'll be angry and broke. It'll eat you up. Accept where you are. Do you want to be happy.

**Sophie**  Of course.

**Chris**  Why of course.

**Sophie**  …

**Chris**  Just accept it. You're on a journey. You don't know the way. Accept it and see beyond money. Spend someone else's. You'll pay it back. When you've found it.

**Sophie**  Found what.

**Chris**  The place where you belong.

*Pause.*

Why did you fall asleep on the tube.

**Sophie**  Well.

**Chris**  You were drunk.

**Sophie**  A little.

**Chris**  Yes. You were alone.

**Sophie**  Yes.

**Chris**  Are you single.

**Sophie**  …No.

**Chris**  So you had a row.

*Beat.*

Yes. Doesn't look very good here does it.

**Sophie** …

**Chris** Relationship fucked up. I haven't heard you mention getting to work. No career to speak of. You try to drown it with drink and some fancy clothes but face it. You're lonely you're broke and your life here is making you so angry.

**Sophie** Who the fuck are you –

**Chris** So angry you nearly tear the head off someone you've never met before.

**Sophie** Jesus.

**Chris** And all over ten lousy pounds.

**Sophie** Look who the fuck are you to talk to me like this.

**Chris** See what I mean.

*Beat.*

Now. Downstairs is the underground. It'll take you back into the city. Up here there's me. I'm outta here. I'm flying out. I've no money and I've no fucking idea what I'm going to do when I get there. But I'm looking. I have nothing here and I'm leaving it behind. I don't know if it's right but I'm doing it. I have a spare ticket.

*Beat.*

Relax.

# Scene 7

*Sushi restaurant.*

*DAVID and KATE sit on stools. A conveyor belt carrying brightly coloured plates and dishes whirrs past them.*

**David** (*Eating.*) Not bad.

**Kate** Yeah.?

*DAVID nods. Eats.*

**David** Shouldn't really be sat in here of course.

*Beat.*

**Kate** Why not.

**David** Japanese.

**Kate** What's wrong with that.

**David** Very brutal people.

**Kate** Many peoples are brutal. Aren't they.

**David** Not like the Japanese. You wouldn't know. Thank God.

**Kate** What. What wouldn't I know.

**David** What they did during the war.

**Kate** Why wouldn't I know that.

**David** Because you weren't there.

**Kate** Neither were you.

*Beat.*

I don't mean that nastily.

**David** No. You just know everything.

**Kate** I do know some things.

**David** You young people.

**Kate** About Japan I mean. I've studied it actually.

**David** Oh

**Kate** Very interesting country.

**David** Interesting. Is that what you call it.

**Kate** Totally different culture to ours.

**David** Never!

**Kate** I'm not an expert. We looked at the idea of the group. I mean the whole. The wishes of the individual being less important than the needs of the group.

**David** Or the system.

**Kate** Well.

**David** The system used to control the group.

**Kate** No. You're seeing it from the wrong perspective.

**David** Don't tell me I'm wrong.

**Kate** I think it's to do with Japanese Buddhism.

**David** Don't call me an idiot.

**Kate** And the importance of order.

**David** I wasn't born yesterday girl.

**Kate** Neither was I.

*Beat.*

**David**  Bloody conveyor belt.

**Kate**  Funny isn't it.

**David**  Funny.

**Kate**  Well have you ever seen this before?

**David**  No.

**Kate**  Well then. It's fun isn't it. And you don't have to wait
for your food you can just pick it up when you
want it.

**David**  You don't have to speak to a human being either do
you.

**Kate**  Yes –

**David**  Oh yes. When you pay.

*Beat.*

We are being replaced.

**Kate**  By the Japanese.

**David**  Someone's got to be responsible.

**Kate**  I'm sorry but you are a racist.

*DAVID laughs. Pause.*

**David**  So where did you learn all this stuff about Japan
then.

**Kate**  On a course.

**David**  Oh on a course. What course.

**Kate**  A business management course.

**David**  Oh.

**Kate**  We learnt about modern theories of the workplace.

**David**  Really.

**Kate**  A lot of it came from Japan. How to motivate staff.

**David**  Not how to treat people.

**Kate**  How to avoid exclusion. Make people feel involved.
Make them feel listened to. Important.

**David**  *Sounds* wonderful.

**Kate**  How important people are the most precious
resources a company has.

**David**  Mmmm.

**Kate**  How we must ask of ourselves: how can I change?
How can I harness the skills of my employees? How
can we work together. Everyone clear on their role. For
a common aim.

**David**  Which is what.

**Kate**  A happier working life.

**David**  To what end.

**Kate**  What.

**David**  Why do we need to be 'happier' at work.

**Kate**  To do our jobs better.

**David**  Yes. To what end.

**Kate**  Increased efficiency.

**David**  Yes and why –

**Kate**  So the company is more competitive.

**David**  Yes! so it can –

**Kate**  So it can make more money. Yes.

**David**  For who.

**Kate**  For the people who own it.

**David**  Yes the shareholders the bosses. Not the workers not ordinary people like me who've shovelled shit –

**Kate**  No! People like me who've worked hard to make their ideas…their dreams…into a reality…

**David**  …

**Kate**  I've worked bloody hard too you're not the only one.

**David**  I don't think I want to hear any more of this.

**Kate**  You wanted to know about me.

**David**  Well I'm not sure I can stand it.

**Kate**  Stand what exactly.

**David**  What you've become.

   *Beat.*

**Kate**  What did you tell me eh.

**David**  What.

**Kate**  When I was a kid when I was growing up you always said I should do whatever made me happy.

**David**  I didn't want to restrict you.

**Kate**  Well I have and now I'm successful and that makes me happy.

**David**  Like I was restricted.

**Kate**  I am in control of my life and yes I am rich. I'm sorry…everybody! Everybody listen! I'm sorry but I have worked hard I still work hard and I am bloody rich. Okay? Sorry. I am rich. And that makes me happy.

**David**  You look it sat here not eating raw fish arguing with your father.

*KATE wiping away tears. Not breaking down.*

Yeah you look it.

**Kate**  I am emotional.

**David**  You look bloody awful.

**Kate**  Thank you. I am fine.

**David**  Oh. Well I'm glad someone is.

**Kate**  Oh please…!

**David**  No no! Good luck to you. You carry on. Fuck everybody else.

**Kate**  No –

**David**  No no you enjoy yourself. People are starving but you come along and pick away in trendy bloody restaurants.

**Kate**  It's not really trendy.

**David**  No no.

**Kate**  It's actually a bit passé.

**David**  Don't try and get out of it. You said it. You've worked hard for everything you've got and you'll be fucked if anyone else is going to get their hands on any of it.

**Kate**  I did not say that.

**David**  Fuck everybody else.

**Kate**  …!

**David**  Don't worry about it.

**Kate**  God…

**David**  Don't worry about me.

**Kate**  Yeah yeah come on.

**David**  What.

**Kate**  This is what this is about isn't it.

**David**  …What?

**Kate**  You. This is all about you isn't it.

**David**  Me!

**Kate**  Look at you. So busy wallowing in your own self-pity.

**David**  What!

**Kate**  Dressing it up as anger against this fighting that.

**David**  How dare you…

**Kate**  What tell the truth. Look at you. Lecturing me. Your whole problem. You'll never accept anything.

**David**  Accept. There you go. That's your motto isn't it. You lot. We accept! We accept anything and everything. We do not reject. Rejecting is bad for business. Well no: I won't accept. I won't accept your world –

**Kate**  You won't accept yourself. You're a lonely useless old man. Shouting at no-one.

**David**  …You

**Kate**  You're redundant. Nobody needs you any more. Accept that.

**David**  You little bitch.

**Kate**  Mum left you because you're a lonely depressive.

**David**  No.

**Kate**  You convert your frustration into anger which you release on those closest to you. You think you're radical and politically… You're just unhappy.

**David**  That is not true.

**Kate**  Isn't it.

**David**  No.

*Pause.*

How dare you.

**Kate**  Yes. I escaped didn't I.

**David**  …What're you talking about.

**Kate**  Home. I got out. How dare I. I left that stinking little town –

**David**  For a stinking big town. Yeah.

*Pause.*

I came down here to patch things up.

*KATE looks then laughs.*

**Kate**  I don't believe you…!

**David**  Kate please.

**Kate**  Oh my God.

**David** What.

**Kate** Did you just…oh God. You need me. Don't you. That's why you came down.

**David** I wanted to –

**Kate** You've nothing left have you. Nothing. Except me. There's nothing in your life is there. Except time. That's all you've got. Plenty of time. And no-one to share it with.

**David** …

**Kate** I wish I could feel sorry for you. But that's what Mum did. Took up most of her life. I'm not going to do it. You came here for you. Not me.

*Beat.*

Take a look at yourself. Or you're going to die a very lonely old man.

*Beat.*

I'm going now. I'm really going. (*She exits.*)

# Scene 8

*Bridge over the river. A slow sunrise under the scene.*

*ALEX and NICK shuffle on. Worse for wear.*

**Nick** (*Stopping.*) No. I'm not going any further.

**Alex** Look it's not far.

**Nick** I don't care.

**Alex** It's just south of the river.

**Nick** I don't want to buy it.

*Beat.*

Look at that water. Fast-flowing sewage. Running right under us.

*ALEX is grimacing, woozy.*

I'm not staying in this place any longer. I want a cab.

**Alex**  What.

**Nick**  I'm going.

**Alex**  ...Right.

**Nick**  You coming.

**Alex**  Well no, I'll... I'm only just down here.

**Nick**  I mean. Are you coming to Cambridge.

*Beat.*

**Alex**  ...What –

**Nick**  I want a decision.

**Alex**  Now.

**Nick**  Why not.

*Beat.*

**Alex**  I need time.

**Nick**  To do what.

**Alex**  Think...

**Nick**  To talk to Ben.

**Alex**  ...Maybe.

**Nick**  Ask him what it's like working for me.

**Alex**  Well. Yes. I suppose.

   *Beat.*

**Nick**  You have to leave it behind.

**Alex**  What.

**Nick**  Friendship.

**Alex**  Do you.

**Nick**  Very liberating. Not having people around you.

**Alex**  Yes. Is it.

**Nick**  Needing you to be something…constant. Holding you down.

   *Beat.*

   You want to make it. Don't you.

**Alex**  …

**Nick**  I mean really make it.

**Alex**  Yes.

**Nick**  Tell me the truth.

**Alex**  Alright.

**Nick**  You've always doubted Ben haven't you.

**Alex**  Yes.

**Nick**  Always known he'll always be serving someone else. A slave.

**Alex**  Yes

**Nick**  A bit of a mug.

**Alex**  Yes.

**Nick**  We're the same you and me.

**Alex**  He's still my friend.

**Nick**  From back home.

**Alex**  Yes.

**Nick**  When did you last call him.

*Beat.*

I don't know when I began to suspect him. To wonder. So anyway. We had a meeting. I confronted him.

**Alex**  With what.

**Nick**  I asked him for a pledge of loyalty.

**Alex**  To the company.

**Nick**  Yes. And to me.

**Alex**  He wouldn't give it.

**Nick**  On the contrary. He gave it without hesitation.

**Alex**  Oh.

**Nick**  Which was precisely the problem.

*ALEX is weary, suffering.*

Look. I need bright people. Bright enough to stab me in the back with their own start-ups. If they can't they're not clever enough.

**Alex**  So…

**Nick**  I need to keep them. Not for long. Just long enough. Two…three years.

**Alex**  And how –

**Nick**  How to keep them. That's your problem.

*Beat.*

**Alex**  So what happened.

**Nick**  I sacked him. Paid him off.

**Alex**  Right.

**Nick**  And I was going to let him go. I really was. Just walk off down the road. But I had to tell him.

**Alex**  Tell him what.

**Nick**  The truth. You know that. If people know the truth they at least have the chance to turn things around. Change. Move on. Whatever.

**Alex**  What did you tell him.

**Nick**  Exactly what I felt. Exactly what you've known about him for years. That he's not up to it. Can't hack it. Not really. Too fucking nice. Whatever that. Really means. Told him straight.

**Alex**  Did you

**Nick**  It's only fair. You've got to be straight with people. I said forget it. It's not going to happen for you. All the time giving him the chance.

**Alex**  To what.

**Nick**  To get rid of himself and become another man.

**Alex**  Another man

**Nick**  If no-one tells you how will you ever know. If you don't know…

*Beat.*

**Alex**  How did he take it.

**Nick**  Very badly.

**Alex**  I'm not surprised.

**Nick**  Very depressed.

**Alex**  You've spoken to / him.

**Nick**  I'd told him everything he needed to know. Why speak to him.

**Alex**  Where is he.

*DAVID wanders on unseen, leans over bridge. ALEX is very shaky.*

**Nick**  I told him. Look around you. There is nothing more to be done. We have done everything.

**Alex**  That is not true.

**Nick**  The only thing left is to make money. Save yourself from the madness. Only the weak and the stupid resist it.

**Alex**  Where is he.

*DAVID is retching. Still unseen.*

**Nick**  Recovering. I think.

**Alex**  How do you mean.

**Nick**  He tried to kill himself.

**Alex**  …?

**Nick**  He made a choice.

**Alex**  He did what.

**Nick**  It may well have been the right one God knows.
Leave it all behind.

**Alex**  He tried to commit suicide.

**Nick**  Yes. Almost immediately. Quite decisive. For him.
And brave I suppose. Thought it may just have been a
cry for…

**Alex**  …You stand here and…

**Nick**  But this is the point.

**Alex**  …!

**Nick**  I have to tell you. I'm giving you the chance. Ben
made me realise. I have a personnel crisis. I need
someone. When I ran into you I remembered. You
impressed me. I watched you. From outside the bar. You
looked like you needed…something. I realised it was
perfect. I needed people of the highest calibre. They
must know the truth and make the only choice there is
to be made. I need someone to find them and keep
them. Who better than you.

*DAVID retching. Sick.*

Your friend is nothing. Nobody really. You knew it. I
told you. He almost destroyed himself. Couldn't
manage that. Now. Having told you that. If you choose
to come and work for me. you will be perfect. You will
embody the company. You will be our mission: to know
the truth and make the only choice possible.

*DAVID being sick.*

Perfect.

**Alex** …

**Nick** Either that or.

**Alex** You.

**Nick** Or you will weaken. Now is the moment. Your whole life. Friendship will weaken and destroy you. You have no choice. Come to Cambridge.

*DAVID is sick. ALEX produces an expensive ballpoint, clicks it open and slashes down the side of NICK's neck.*

**Nick** Oh dear.

**Alex** You…fuck you!

**Nick** How weak you are.

**Alex** Cunt I'll kill you.

*NICK has fallen. ALEX stops attack.*

**Nick** How predictable.

*DAVID has been watching. As ALEX stumbles off, he grabs him.*

**Alex** Get the fuck off me old man.

**David** Oi just fucking…

*They are struggling.*

Calm down.

**Alex** Let go of me.

**David** You just. You've. You've fucking killed him.

**Alex** Who are you Robin Hood.

**David** Maybe I am.

**Alex**  Can't you fuck off and mind your own.

**David**  Yeah and if we all do that

**Alex**  He deserved it. He was a cunt.

**David**  So you're Robin Hood.

**Alex**  Maybe.

*Beat.*

**David**  It's not right

**Alex**  It felt right.

**David**  Can't just do what you feel. All the time though. Can you.

**Alex**  Why not.

**David**  Things like this happen.

**Alex**  Things like this happen all the time.

**David**  Well. They have to be answered for. Somebody has to.

**Alex**  (*Laughs.*) Not from round here are you.

**David**  No. Thank God.

*Beat.*

He was someone's son. You thought of that. Ever had a son.

**Alex**  I've had a father.

**David**  There's no way you can understand. You know nothing about it.

**Alex**  You sound just like him. Fathers. Fuck them.

**David**  And everybody else. Yeah.

**Alex**  What do they give you.

**David**  They try their best.

**Alex**  Their bitterness. Lies.

**David**  They've seen the way the world works.

**Alex**  How to be scared. How to hate. Make money.

**David**  They're only human.

**Alex**  They teach you nothing.

**David**  Maybe they've learnt nothing.

**Alex**  Then they've failed.

*Beat.*

**David**  (*NICK.*) Someone's son. Someone's. Baby.

**Alex**  (*Rage.*) I'm never going to have kids. I'd rather die. I've nothing to give them.

**David**  Nothing.

**Alex**  Just what he gave me. Anger. And cash. Plenty of cash. I wouldn't give that to anybody.

*DAVID lets ALEX go.*

**Alex**  What's wrong with you.

**David**  Go on fuck off.

**Alex**  What.

**David**  Go on.

*Beat.*

You won't get far.

**Alex**  What's going to stop me. (*Shouts.*) Hey you lot look! Hey! Over here! I just killed somebody! Yeah! Me! I'm a killer!

*Beat.*

Look. They don't care.

**David**  They're scared.

**Alex**  They're not listening. You shout in this town and people think you're messing about. Having fun. Or mad. They leave you alone.

**David**  You are fucked.

**Alex**  You're wrong. I'm high.

**David**  You're panicking. You're in shock.

**Alex**  I'm delirious.

**David**  Accept it. Look at it. What you've done.

**Alex**  I want to dance.

**David**  It'll ruin you.

**Alex**  I've done a great thing. The best thing. I've ever done.

*Beat.*

**David**  You're going nowhere.

**Alex**  I'll do what I like.

*ALEX laughs. DAVID grabs to restrain. ALEX laughing harder. DAVID practically throttling.*

**David**  Fucking nutter. Can't you see. You need help. You need saving. From yourself.

84

**Alex** (*Hysterical. Shouts.*) Help! Help police! Help! There's a murderer here! Help! Murder! (*Laughing.*) Somebody! Please help! Anybody!

**David** Shut it. Shut up.

*ALEX overpowers DAVID. Kicks him hard.*

**Alex** No. You shut up. You. Shut the fuck up.

*ALEX wanders off. DAVID raises his head to see him, watching him go. His head drops again. He raises his head once more, then slams it into the ground. A beat. Raises his head, does the same again.*

# Scene 9

*Hut.*

*SOPHIE and CHRIS lie in bed.*

**Sophie** Mmm.

**Chris** Yeah?

**Sophie** Yeah.

**Chris** Oh. Good.

**Sophie** That was…amazing.

**Chris** Great.

**Sophie** I mean that was…yeah.

**Chris** Was it.

**Sophie** Yeah. I was. Off. Somewhere. Somewhere else.

**Chris** …Really.

**Sophie** Oh yeah.

**Chris**  Good. Great.

**Sophie**  …Mmm.

*Beat.*

What time is it.

**Chris**  God knows.

*Beat.*

**Sophie**  So hot.

**Chris**  Yeah. Great thing is here…when it rains it rains. When it's hot it's hot.

**Sophie**  Oh.

**Chris**  So I hear.

**Sophie**  I like the sound of that.

**Chris**  Yeah.

**Sophie**  Always seems to be half-way back at home. Like sunny but cloudy too. Or rainy but windy and it's always changing.

**Chris**  Right.

**Sophie**  You never know where you are.

**Chris**  Can't relax into the mood of a day.

**Sophie**  Yes. Yes exactly.

*Beat.*

**Chris**  So what're we going to do. We're here. I mean we could do some exploring. Find a bar.

**Sophie**  Listen.

**Chris** Find somewhere to…

**Sophie** Aren't you hungry.

**Chris** …Yeah. Yeah sure.

**Sophie** Me too.

**Chris** Fuck I'm starving. Let's go eat. I'll get my card.

**Sophie** Look why don't we just try not to go too mad. Just see how we go. For a bit.

**Chris** Okay.

**Sophie** I'm not exactly…flush.

**Chris** I could get it. But. Cool cool. I could make something.

**Sophie** …Yeah.

**Chris** Yeah I'll scout round. There must be a market of some kind.

**Sophie** Yeah there must be something. I can change some money and / give you some cash.

**Chris** No don't be silly

**Sophie** Look it's fine. I'll need to sometime

**Chris** No no honestly

**Sophie** I will though won't I

**Chris** Yeah. You get the next / lot

**Sophie** Yeah I will

**Chris** Whatever

**Sophie** No I will

**Chris**  Okay.

*Beat.*

No cooker. Course. And no… (*Looking for crockery etc.*)
No. I've got some. Bits and pieces. Shit I'm thirsty.

**Sophie**  Is the water okay.

**Chris**  Don't know. Don't reckon. Fuck knows.

*Beat.*

I've got a towel and stuff.

**Sophie**  Okay.

*Beat.*

**Chris**  Shall I open this. (*He opens doors, goes onto the balcony. Stands.*)

**Sophie**  Can you see the ocean.

**Chris**  Not quite. Breeze is nice though.

**Sophie**  What.

**Chris**  I said the breeze is nice.

*Beat.*

**Sophie**  (*Getting up.*) Yeah…?

**Chris**  (*Not turning round.*) Don't get up.

*SOPHIE stays.*

I didn't think you'd do it. Didn't think you'd come. I've
met loads of girls. Girls who said they'd love to just take
off. Or they've been off before and they need to go
again. Pissed. Parties. Whatever. They never do. They
never have. I didn't think you'd come.

**Sophie**  (*Quiet.*) I had to do something.

**Chris**  God. You looked gorgeous. At the airport. All messy. But gorgeous. That's how you know when someone's really lovely. They look sexy with sleep in their eyes.

*CHRIS turns. They look at each other.*

Sorry. I'm a bit of a weirdo.

*They smile.*

**Sophie**  Funny

**Chris**  What

**Sophie**  Empty

**Chris**  Yeah

**Sophie**  So much space

**Chris**  Gorgeous.

**Sophie**  Bit scary.

**Chris**  Is it.

**Sophie**  Well.

**Chris**  No. It's brilliant. Makes you realise.

**Sophie**  What.

**Chris**  What's important. In a room. When there's nothing.

**Sophie**  Things are nice though.

**Chris**  When there's only people.

**Sophie**  Aren't they. Sometimes.

**Chris**  It's the people that are important. Not the things.

**Sophie**  Yeah. Yeah of course.

*Beat.*

**Chris**  What.

**Sophie**  …?

**Chris**  Have I said something.

**Sophie**  What do you mean.

**Chris**  You okay

**Sophie**  …Yeah

**Chris**  Right.

**Sophie**  What

**Chris**  It's just sometimes…

**Sophie**  …What.

**Chris**  Sometimes I'm not sure what you're thinking.

**Sophie**  Sometimes I'm not thinking anything.

**Chris**  Right.

**Sophie**  Like now.

**Chris**  Okay.

*Beat.*

You can be a bit quiet.

**Sophie**  Normally I don't shut up. Back home. I talk shit almost constantly.

*CHRIS laughs. Beat.*

**Chris**  Maybe we should find a bar. Have a beer. I can get it. I need a drink. Yeah?

**Sophie**  …Well okay

**Chris**  You don't want to

**Sophie**  …Sorry?

**Chris**  You don't want to go out. For a drink.

**Sophie**  I just said yes

**Chris**  I like bars. I like beer. When I have a couple of beers it slows me down. I can talk. There's nothing wrong with that is there.

**Sophie**  No. It's natural.

> *Beat.*

Aren't you hungry.

**Chris**  We can have something in the bar.

**Sophie**  Right. Okay.

**Chris**  You don't want to do you. It's okay. You can say.

**Sophie**  I know.

**Chris**  You stay here. Back to plan A. I'll scout round. Find something.

**Sophie**  …

**Chris**  Sorry I'm being weird.

**Sophie**  I don't really mind. What we do.

**Chris**  Okay

**Sophie**  But we should eat

**Chris**  Yeah

**Sophie**  And yes I'd like a drink.

**Chris**  Cool

**Sophie**  I'd want some water

**Chris**  Yeah

**Sophie**  And then I'd like a beer.

**Chris**  Cool.

*Beat.*

Okay.

*CHRIS goes to his rucksack, starts finding clothes. SOPHIE goes to her carrier bags, takes out some inappropriate clothes. Then she finds her mobile. Starts fiddling with it. CHRIS sees, takes it from her suddenly.*

Ah ah ah.

*Beat.*

**Sophie**  What you doing.

**Chris**  Don't you think you should

**Sophie**  What.

**Chris**  Well. Wait a bit.

**Sophie**  Wait a bit

**Chris**  Before. Contacting anyone.

**Sophie**  …Can I have my phone.

*CHRIS puts it behind his back.*

**Chris**  I think you should. Try it. See how long you can go.

*SOPHIE half smiles, holds out her hand.*

I haven't got it.

**Sophie**  …

**Chris**  (*Holds out a hand.*) See

**Sophie**  Come on

**Chris**  (*Other hand.*) Honest.

**Sophie**  Can you just give me my phone.

*Beat. CHRIS gives it to her.*

Thanks.

*SOPHIE wanders off, dialling. CHRIS watches. SOPHIE waits.*

Hello. Hello? Oh my god hello. It's me. My God I can't believe. Hello? (*She looks at CHRIS. Mouths.*) My sister.

*CHRIS half nods.*

Hello hi lost you there. Where are you. Hello. Fuck. Hello.

*CHRIS is watching.*

Oh for Christs's – hello. Where are you the reception's terrible. What? (*Half to CHRIS.*) I think she's off her face. What? (*Laughs.*) Guess what. Guess where I am… No. No fuck off. Listen. I'm – hello. HELLO. Jesus. Yeah hello I'm travelling yeah I thought fuck it. Yeah I know you're travelling. She's off her face. Listen I'm travelling too. Where are you. Hello. (*Screams.*) Yes. I'm travelling. Where are you. Fuck. (*Looks at mobile.*) Oh fuck the fucking… (*Back to her ear.*) Hello. (*Looks at it again.*) The fucking battery's… (*Back to her ear.*) Hello.

*Suddenly CHRIS takes it from her and smashes it on the floor. Beat.*

What are you doing.

**Chris**  Just listen okay just listen

**Sophie**  That was my sister.

**Chris**  Look I'm sorry I fucked up I know that was…

**Sophie**  What are you doing.

**Chris**  Listen if you let go you've got to let go. You can't. I'm sorry but. You said fuck it. You have to. Don't fight it. Don't try to. You know? You're like me. Aren't you.

**Sophie**  …I don't know…

**Chris**  I saw you and straight away I thought. You're like me you don't know where you are you haven't got a clue what you want. You feel fucked. And. You've got. Nothing. Nothing definite. Nothing forever. And that's crazy. But it's amazing. If you don't fight it.

*Beat. CHRIS starts to cry.*

I'm sorry. I got angry. I don't mean to. I'm sorry. But. I'm tired. I'm fucked. I'm hungry. I want a beer. I need to eat.

*Beat.*

Look. I'm lost. And you're lost. But. I'm looking. And you said fuck it. You said I'm lost. Didn't you.

**Sophie**  …I don't know…

**Chris**  You said I'm lost and I want to look. So be lost. Go with it. And look. With me.

*Beat.*

I'm sorry. Look. I'll. I'll go and. I'll find us something. I'm fucked. We need to eat.

**Sophie**  No.

94

**Chris**  No I will.

**Sophie**  No it's alright. I can go.

>   *Beat.*

>   You're right. Everything you said. You're right.

>   *Beat.*

>   We can talk. Later. But we need to eat. And some drink. Something to drink.

>   *Beat.*

>   You're exhausted. It's okay. I can go.

>   *Beat.*

>   It's alright. Really. I can go.

# Scene 10

*Cell / interview room.*

*ALEX sits. DANNY stands.*

**Danny**  Thirsty. Want a fag. Here.

>   *Beat.*

>   I'll have one. Shouldn't. Still. (*Lights fag.*) Little bit of what you fancy. Can't hurt.

>   *Pause.*

>   I said d'you want a coffee or something. Listen mate you try anything don't you worry. Uniforms through that door. Flood of black and white. Kick your teeth in for you before you even get up. See this bleeper. Silicon. Connected. In there mate. So don't even.

*Beat.*

You're quiet. I can tell. They're either quiet or trappy. When they're in the shit. I know. I've seen them. You're quiet.

**Alex** I'm thinking.

**Danny** I've never done a murderer.

**Alex** Who are you again.

*Pause.*

**Danny** You aren't rich that's obvious. I mean stinking. I wouldn't be here. He'd be straight out of bed and right up your arse. Wouldn't he.

**Alex** Who.

**Danny** Your brief.

**Alex** And you're a brief's lackey.

**Danny** I work for myself thank you. I'm sub-contracted.

*Beat.*

I can be important though. Make sure the boys don't try it on. Oh yeah. Fuck you right over the law can. I know them down here. Know them all.

*Beat.*

Some people are very kind. Very grateful. For my help. He could be a while see.

**Alex** My brief.

**Danny** He could be a she. Whatever.

*Beat.*

I've got friends as well. Paper friends. Could write this up. What's happening here. Write it up like a story. Could be worth something. Could be worth a fuck of a lot. Should you go down. Not much of a story otherwise. (*Laughs.*) Could sort you out. For a bit. Worth less and less isn't it.

**Alex** Thank you. I'll bear that in mind.

**Danny** You got any money have you. I mean in general. It does help let's face it.

**Alex** I have some.

**Danny** Good how much.

**Alex** …

**Danny** I hope you've got tons. For your sake. Expensive business justice.

*Pause.*

**Alex** Do you think they'll let me see someone.

**Danny** Your woman.

**Alex** No.

**Danny** Man. Whatever. Not that I care.

**Alex** Then why do you ask.

**Danny** Pass the time.

*Beat.*

**Alex** A friend.

**Danny** Has he got any money.

**Alex** I don't know.

**Danny**  Those are the friends you want. Right now.

**Alex**  A friend from home. Will they let me see him.

**Danny**  I have no idea.

*Pause.*

Tell me what it's like.

**Alex**  What. (*Exactly.*)

**Danny**  You kicked that cunt to death I heard. Ripped the other one's neck in half. Poor fucker. How did it look. When you did it. Is blood really the colour it is in films. Or on telly. Or is it darker. Did you enjoy it. Did it make you chuck. Or what.

*Beat.*

Why did you do it. Were you a bad kid. Did your Dad fuck you up. What was going through your head. I have to know. Come on you cunt who d'you think you are. I'm in charge of you now you fucking tell me what I need to know alright.

*Beat.*

Funny. You seem like a nice boy.

*Beat. ALEX looks at DANNY. They look at each other for a moment.*

**Alex**  Who are you.

**Danny**  I act. I'm waiting to act. I do this in between. Wait with the apprehended. The charged. The innocent. The guilty. Whatever. You're entitled. It's the law. Until your brief gets out of bed. Out of the pub. The casino. I do a lot of different things. Allsorts. Everybody's got to eat.

98

*Beat.*

Tell me what it was like. I might need to know one day.
I've never done a murderer. I seem to do coppers. Small
ones. Cough and a spit. As they say. But one day I will.
One day I'll make it and do a murderer. Place just
outside the smoke. Travel in for meetings. For
murderers. I'll be famous.

*Beat.*

I need to know. How did it feel. For when my day
comes. My break. Tell me.

**Alex**  I don't remember.

*A knock at the door.*

**Danny**  Expecting anyone.

*ALEX looks at him. Another knock. DANNY goes out through
the door. Pause. ALEX starts to look up for a camera. DANNY
enters holding a mobile.*

Desk sergeant was just popping this into plastic it
started ringing. Typical filth. Couldn't keep his nose out.
Must be something good. Highly irregular. Allowing
this sort of contact.

*Beat.*

D'you want me to take it.

*ALEX holds out his hand.*

(*Into phone.*) He's just here sweetheart. (*He passes the phone
to ALEX. Mouths.*) They. Are. Listening.

*Half a beat.*

Probably.

*ALEX takes the phone. Lights on SOPHIE on a payphone, another part of the stage.*

*Beat.*

**Alex**  Hello.

**Sophie**  Hi. Where are you.

**Alex**  Sophie. I can't say.

**Sophie**  What?

**Alex**  …?

**Sophie**  Can you not talk.

**Alex**  Yeah

**Sophie**  Is there someone there.

*ALEX looks at DANNY, who retreats but stays.*

**Alex**  No. Not really

*Beat.*

Where are you.

**Sophie**  I haven't got long. Listen I came away on a flight.

**Alex**  Away

**Sophie**  Yeah and I need to get back I'm sorry to call you like this

**Alex**  How do you mean you've gone away.

**Sophie**  Look I haven't got time I'm phoning because they stopped my limit

*Beat.*

Hello.

**Alex**  You want money.

**Sophie**  I need to get back I can't explain now

**Alex**  …?

**Sophie**  Look I'm sorry I'm just really desperate I've got this ticket it takes you round the world somehow but you have to go one-way. You can't go back on yourself

**Alex**  Why did you buy it.

**Sophie**  I didn't. Look it was an impulse a moment kind of

**Alex**  You went away. Just like that.

**Sophie**  I needed to do something please don't judge me not now

**Alex**  You want my number. My card.

**Sophie**  Yes. Please. You'll get it back.

**Alex**  Where are you exactly

**Sophie**  For fuck's sake. There's not much money left on the phone I don't have any more. I need your number now please.

**Alex**  I can't get my card.

**Sophie**  What.

**Alex**  I can't get it.

**Sophie**  What do you mean. Where are you. I spoke to someone but

**Alex**  Will you help me.

**Sophie**  Jesus!

**Alex**  Will you. Will you help me

**Sophie**  Of course I'll help you of course but

**Alex**  I mean whatever

**Sophie**  …! Yes

**Alex**  I've done something. You have to help me. I'm going mad and it's not even started

**Sophie**  Alex where are you

**Alex**  Don't

**Sophie**  What

**Alex**  (*Struggling.*) Don't say my name. I won't be able to. If you say my name.

**Sophie**  Alright I won't but you have to fucking hurry up and help me because the money is running out

**Alex**  The money

**Sophie**  Yes the money

**Alex**  Is that all you want

**Sophie**  What

**Alex**  The money

**Sophie**  No I want to come back I want to sort things out

**Alex**  Sort things out

**Sophie**  Yes I want to

*Beat.*

I don't know I don't know what. Can you just

**Alex**  Give you the number

**Sophie**  Yes

**Alex**  Give you the money

**Sophie**  Yes

**Alex**  I don't know

**Sophie**  …! (*She bangs the phone hard into the wall. Breathes.*)

**Alex**  Do you love me.

*She listens again.*

**Sophie**  What.

**Alex**  Do you love me.

**Sophie**  …

**Alex**  Do you.

**Sophie**  I think so.

**Alex**  …

**Sophie**  I don't know

**Alex**  …

**Sophie**  Alex

**Alex**  Don't.

**Sophie**  …

**Alex**  …The truth is. Neither do I.

**Sophie**  …

**Alex**  How can we sort things out. How can we. If we don't know.

**Sophie**  Alex I'm scared. Tell me what's happened.

**Alex**  We can't sort this out

**Sophie**  …The phone

**Alex**  We can't it's too big

**Sophie**  (*Rage.*) Tell me

**Alex**  Not without love. Without knowing

**Sophie**  Look will you tell me will you just fucking tell me

**Alex**  I've killed.

**Sophie**  …What.

**Alex**  I think I've killed.

**Sophie**  …

**Alex**  I have. If you're listening. I don't care. I've killed. Twice.

**Sophie**  …

**Alex**  And I'm not sure. Why. Do you understand.

**Sophie**  …Alex

**Alex**  Don't. Use. My fucking. Name.

**Sophie**  …No. I don't understand.

**Alex**  Neither do I.

**Sophie**  (*Phone.*) Oh Christ it's going.

**Alex**  Maybe you should just use it.

**Sophie**  It's…

**Alex**  Use your ticket.

**Sophie**  It's gone…gone.

**Alex**  Follow your own path.

*The phone is dead. SOPHIE stands. Lights fade on her.*
*ALEX puts the phone on the table. Beat. DANNY goes and*
*picks it up. He looks at ALEX*

# Scene 11

*Graveyard.*

*KATE and DANNY stand waiting.*

**Kate**  I'm not sure if I should use you.

**Danny**  Well make up your mind.

**Kate**  It's alright there's time.

**Danny**  I don't do this for love / you know.

**Kate**  You'll get your money whatever. Okay!

*Beat.*

I used to want to piss everybody off. Mix it up a bit.

**Danny**  Really.

**Kate**  Turn up to things alone on purpose. Make them all
talk. Feeling really bad I'd bring a friend. A girl I mean.
Hold hands. Should've seen their faces.

*Beat.*

Not sure I can be bothered anymore.

**Danny**  Well can you just hurry up –

**Kate**  Look you'll get your fucking money whether I use
you or not but only I said ONLY if you shut up and do
exactly what I say.

**Danny**  Yes ma'am.

*Beat.*

**Kate**  Don't really want to stand out anymore. Too much trouble. Want them all to leave me alone. Get it done. Get home.

**Danny**  Your family…

**Kate**  I'm not really talking *to* you.

**Danny**  Should I listen.

**Kate**  Yes. I mean I don't really care anymore. I don't want to upset them. What's the point. They don't do anything anyway. They don't care. Anyway. Suppose I'm a bit older.

*Beat.*

**Danny**  Can I ask you something.

**Kate**  Yes.

**Danny**  Tell me who I am. Just in case.

**Kate**  You're my…man…friend.

**Danny**  …Boyfriend?

**Kate**  Partner. Whatever.

**Danny**  And how long…

**Kate**  I'm not sure. Not a long time. Not a short time.

**Danny**  We're happy?

**Kate**  Yes.

**Danny**  But not settled down.

**Kate**  No. We have our own lives.

**Danny**  Presumably I'm successful.

**Kate**  Yes.

**Danny**  Financial…?

**Kate**  No something clever. But caring. But not too obvious.

**Danny**  Everybody's a doctor nowadays.

**Kate**  Exactly.

**Danny**  So…

**Kate**  Perhaps a psychologist.

**Danny**  I like that.

**Kate**  But it needs to be modern. Softer.

**Danny**  Invent something. Give it a name and it exists.

**Kate**  …What?

**Danny**  I am a creative psychologist.

**Kate**  Are you. What's that.

**Danny**  Exactly. Impressive. Wide. Beyond question.

**Kate**  You've a talent for this. I'm not sure if that's good or bad.

**Danny**  Whatever. It's my life.

*Beat.*

So who's dead.

**Kate**  My father.

**Danny**  Did I like him.

**Kate**  …

**Danny**  I mean did we get on.

**Kate**  Perhaps you'd never met.

**Danny**  We might have spoken.

**Kate**  On the phone.

**Danny**  Yes. That's very likely.

**Kate**  You were always so busy.

**Danny**  Still am.

**Kate**  Yes.

**Danny**  Travelling all over the shop.

**Kate**  To international conferences.

**Danny**  Yes. I like that.

**Kate**  You just missed each other somehow.

**Danny**  A shame. Sad.

**Kate**  Yes. You had some nice chats though.

**Danny**  He approved.

**Kate**  I thought so. You could never be sure.

**Danny**  He was a man of few words.

**Kate**  No…no.

**Danny**  Oh.

> *Pause.*

> Should I comfort you.

**Kate**  I've decided I'm not going to be emotional.

**Danny**  Right. Hand round the shoulder.

**Kate**  No.

**Danny** Elbow?

**Kate** No.

**Danny** Right. Problem is…

**Kate** What.

**Danny** Makes me look awful. Right cold bastard.

**Kate** No. It's me being strong.

**Danny** Is it.

**Kate** And you're respecting my space. And my right to behave as I wish on the day of…whatever.

**Danny** I see.

*Beat.*

Was he a big man.

**Kate** Look! Just. Feel your way. Okay.

**Danny** Fine.

**Kate** Do what everybody else is doing.

**Danny** Alright.

**Kate** Just…follow…whatever –

**Danny** Improvise.

**Kate** Yes. Exactly. Yes.

*Pause.*

Do we have to – I'm not talking *to* you just listen – do we have to throw earth I wonder. You always see people throwing earth in don't you. On films or… I don't want to do that.

*Beat.*

I might use you again you know. For other things.

**Danny**  Really.

**Kate**  If this goes off okay.

**Danny**  I'm quite busy.

**Kate**  I'd book you. Reserve you in advance.

**Danny**  I'd need some sort of deposit. Security.

**Kate**  Probably for business. You know. Socialising. Stop the tongues. Or start them. Depending on the occasion. The market.

*Beat.*

Are you around later.

**Danny**  I'm afraid I'm filming.

**Kate**  Okay.

**Danny**  I went for a copper. Three lines. Didn't get them but they must have liked me.

**Kate**  Okay.

**Danny**  Gave me this other character.

**Kate**  I'm afraid you're talking about yourself again. Here come the cars.

*KATE looks in their direction. Starts crying. Not breaking down.*

Isn't black the most beautiful colour.

**Danny**  Are you alright.

**Kate** Don't fucking talk to me yet!

**Danny** I'm trying to get into it.

**Kate** Wait for the people.

**Danny** I'm trying to feel my way in. I'm trying to be professional.

**Kate** Well try without talking. Try without doing anything. Just wait for the cars.

*Blackout.*

# Scene 12

*Hospital.*

*BEN in bed. ALEX hand-cuffed.*

**Alex** I think you're supposed to ask about the food aren't you. In these situations.

**Ben** Yes I think you are.

**Alex** So how is the food.

**Ben** I haven't had any yet.

**Alex** Oh.

**Ben** (*Drip.*) They've got me on this thing.

**Alex** Oh Christ of course.

**Ben** Keeps me going.

**Alex** Stupid stupid fool.

**Ben** It's quite alright.

**Alex** I'm sorry.

**Ben** Really. It's not a problem.

*Beat.*

I haven't seen you for a very long time have I…

**Alex**  Ages. God knows. I don't get home too much.

**Ben**  Neither did I until I tried to kill myself.

*Beat. ALEX looks out of the window.*

**Alex**  Doesn't matter how far you go. You always come back to the sea.

**Ben**  Do you.

**Alex**  (*Smiles.*) So they say.

*BEN smiles.*

I miss it you know.

**Ben**  You miss the sea.

**Alex**  Yeah. The noise of it. Under everything.

**Ben**  It is calming isn't it.

**Alex**  I should get some shells. Take them with me. Whenever I need it. Just –

*ALEX mimes clamping shells over ears. BEN smiles.*

**Ben**  Then you could hear the sea.

**Alex**  Yeah

**Ben**  Wherever you were

**Alex**  Up in the smoke

**Ben**  You'd be back home

**Alex**  Just like that

**Ben**  Two shells.

*They smile.*

It was wrong what you did.

**Alex**  …

**Ben**  You stopped life.

**Alex**  It didn't feel wrong.

**Ben**  But be honest. If you think about it. It's really not the right thing to do.

**Alex**  What about him. What he did.

**Ben**  He was a businessman.

**Alex**  Think about it.

**Ben**  Businessmen have to operate in certain ways.

**Alex**  What he did to you.

**Ben**  He terminated my contract because he no longer felt –

**Alex**  Look at you.

**Ben**  I did this to myself.

**Alex**  But why. For a reason.

*Beat.*

**Ben**  I tried to end my own life. I have to accept that.

**Alex**  You did it for a reason.

**Ben**  I have to deal with it and move on.

**Alex**  Yes. But why did you do it.

**Ben**  I've always had low self-esteem. I don't think I've admitted it.

**Alex**  You were brilliant. Always.

**Ben**  Thinking about when I was young, my development. There were a lot of problems.

**Alex**  Ben please.

**Ben**  I'm not sure I've dealt with all my issues from home.

**Alex**  Join the world.

*Beat.*

Ben. I'm sorry.

**Ben**  It's fine. You're upset.

**Alex**  I just want you to tell me why…

**Ben**  Why I tried to kill myself. It's okay to say it.

**Alex**  Yes.

**Ben**  Personal issues that were unresolved came to the surface.

**Alex**  …! Because…

**Ben**  I was at home too much. Had far too much time to think. I wasn't getting out. Didn't have any money to spend. Stopped…functioning really.

**Alex**  You'd been cast aside.

**Ben**  I'd failed to accept the fact that I was no longer needed.

**Alex**  …!

**Ben**  It's a mindset thing.

**Alex**  Is it.

**Ben**  I could have seen it as a beginning. I could have used it. To change direction completely. Gone away for a while. Whatever. I didn't. I trapped myself by dwelling on the negative.

*Pause.*

Alex. You know, when we were kids. Neither of us had it easy. I mean emotionally.

**Alex**  (*Smiling.*) Emotionally easy…

**Ben**  This town. I'm not sure where the line is.

**Alex**  What line.

**Ben**  I mean. I'm trying to work out where abuse starts –

**Alex**  Oh Jesus Ben.

**Ben**  You're laughing. But what about in your house.

**Alex**  It wasn't that bad –

**Ben**  So why did you get away as quick as you could. Why did I.

**Alex**  We wanted something better.

**Ben**  Something else.

*Beat.*

**Alex**  It wasn't right. What he did.

**Ben**  The world isn't right. Accept that. Change what you can. Change yourself.

**Alex**  And let the world do what it likes.

**Ben**  It will do anyway.

*Beat.*

Upset. Anger. Where does it get you.

**Alex** Right here.

*ALEX indicates his gut. Pause.*

We should fuck off. I mean an escape committee.

**Ben** Should we.

**Alex** Yeah dig a tunnel. Hide the earth. Big bike.
Whatever.

**Ben** Oh. I see. The film.

**Alex** I could dress up as a doctor and wheel you out of
here.

**Ben** I think people might notice.

**Alex** What the shock of seeing a doctor.

*BEN smiles.*

Bit out of the ordinary.

*Beat.*

And there'd be a chase.

**Ben** Would there.

**Alex** There has to be a chase.

**Ben** Oh.

**Alex** There's always a chase. Of some sort. And it would
look like there was no way we were going to do it.

**Ben** Do what.

**Alex** Escape of course. No way we were going to…

**Ben** Right.

**Alex** But of course we would.

**Ben** Would we.

**Alex** Of course. we'd have to. Somehow. We'd have to get away.

**Ben** Oh.

**Alex** Can't bring people down. Have to go home happy.

*Pause.*

**Ben** That was fun wasn't it. Imagining that for those few moments.

**Alex** I mean it. Come on. Let's go. Let's get out of here.

*BEN smiles.*

Don't smile at me you cunt I'm giving you an option here. We'll get out the window. Down on the beach. We could dance. Come on. There'll be a boat. We'll shout it over.

**Ben** And if there's no boat.

**Alex** We'll steal an ambulance. Fuck it. Drive to the airport.

**Ben** And do what.

**Alex** Get away.

*Beat.*

Come on.

*ALEX crying now perhaps. Not breaking down.*

COME ON.

**Ben**  Alex you're upset. That's natural.

**Alex**  COME ON.

**Ben**  But you're still here. You're not dead. Accept that. Accept where you are.

**Alex**  …

**Ben**  Move on. Move forward. You will. You can. I believe in you.

**Alex**  COME ON!

*Pause.*

**Ben**  Alex. I have to take my medicine now.

*ALEX nods. He stands.*

**Alex**  Ben

**Ben**  Yeah.

**Alex**  …I don't know

**Ben**  You wanted to say something

**Alex**  Yeah

**Ben**  What was it.

**Alex**  I don't know. There must be something –

**Ben**  Must there.

**Alex**  All this shit's happened. There must be something to say.

**Ben**  Must there.

*Beat.*

What.

**Alex**  I don't know.

**Ben**  Me neither.

*Beat.*

Let's say goodbye.

**Alex**  Yeah. Okay.

**Ben**  Goodbye.

**Alex**  Goodbye.

*Beat.*

**Ben**  Let me know how you are.

*They look at each other.*